English All Over the Place

GERRY W. ABBOTT has a B.A. from Uni
and a Ph.D. from the University of Manchester. For many years
and in many places he lectured on English and the teaching of it.
His publications include respected works on reading, writing,
grammar and related topics.

ROBERT A. JORDAN has a B.A. from St John's College, Cambridge,
and a Ph.D. from the University of Manchester. He was for many
years an officer of the British Council and a lecturer on education
here and abroad. He is the author of many English language
teaching books useful to both students and teachers.

English All Over the Place

EXPERIENCES WHILE TEACHING ABROAD

by

Gerry Abbott & Bob Jordan

Starhaven

© Part I, Gerry Abbott 2001
© Part II, Bob Jordan 2001
ISBN 0-936315-15-6

Starhaven
42 Frognal, London NW3 6AG
Tel: 020 7435 8724 Fax: 020 7435 4169
In US, c/o Box 2573, La Jolla, CA 92038, USA
email: starhaven@aesthesia.co.uk

Designed and set in Poppl-Pontifex by John Mallinson.
Printed and bound by
CPI Copyspeed, 38 Ballard's Lane, London N3 2BJ.

CONTENTS

Foreword   i
Acknowledgements   iv

Part I: Gerry Abbott   1
1. "Mekong!" (Thailand, 1959)   2
2. The caves of Petchaburi (Thailand, 1960)   7
3. Two bridges (Thailand & Cambodia, 1962)   14
4. Delivered by hand (Hungary, 1963)   21
5. Two kinds of cowardice (Uganda & Kenya, 1972)   28
6. Danny (Uganda, 1972)   33
7. Nowhere to turn (P.D.R.Yemen, 1973)   39
8. Aboard a burning plane (Sabah, 1978)   45
9. Zibethinus! (Sarawak, 1981)   53
10. Going to work in Mandalay (Burma, 1987)   59
11. From elephants to ants (Burma, 1987)   64
12. Eight, eight, eighty-eight (Burma, 1988)   69
13. Here and there, now and then: a postscript   74

Part II: Bob Jordan   79
1. Off the beaten track (Finland, 1961)   80
2. Living with the Cold War (Finland/USSR, 1961-2)   89
3. First posting (Nepal, 1965)   96
4. Hush Puppies to the rescue (Nepal, 1965)   103
5. The bank manager (Nepal, 1965)   107
6. Encounters with animals (Nepal, 1966-67)   110
7. The end of the line (Nepal, 1966)   115
8. Seeking the Spiny Babbler (Nepal, 1967)   120
9. On top of the world (Nepal, 1968)   124
10. New broom sweeps clean (Sierra Leone, 1970)   133
11. Nothing but music (Sierra Leone, 1971)   138
12. The centre of attention (Portugal, 1978)   142
13. Work with a difference (China, 1979)   146
14. We shall overcome (Greece, 1982)   151
15. As others see us: a postscript   156

Foreword

In the 20th century a number of well-known British authors at one time or another taught English abroad to earn a living – E. M. Forster, James Joyce, Wilfred Owen, Lawrence Durrell, Anthony Burgess, John Fowles and Paul Theroux to name but a few. All had made use of their experiences in their writing. Having retired at the same time from teaching English as a foreign language (EFL), we asked ourselves whether we shouldn't make our own small attempt to follow in these distinguished footsteps.

Like many other EFL teachers, we spent much of our time overseas under the auspices of The British Council, a body created in 1934 and given a Royal Charter in 1940. The Council is Britain's principal agency for cultural relations overseas. Today it has offices and/or libraries in more than a hundred countries. It has been instrumental in helping to develop postgraduate courses in English language teaching (ELT) in a number of British universities and sent people like us overseas as teachers, teacher-trainers and even trainers of teacher-trainers. When its emissaries arrive and are asked who they are working for, the questioner sometimes understands the answer as 'The British Consul'. This misunderstanding has more than once worked in our favour by opening doors, ushering us past long queues and cutting red tape.

Like most speakers of English, we have grown accustomed to the fact that our language is now being used all over the world as a medium of global communication. We knew that this did not happen overnight, but we were surprised to come across this observation in a book written by a voyager well before World War I:

> In Japan most of the tradespeople spoke English. At Shanghai, at Hong Kong, at Singapore, at Penang, at Colombo, at Suez, at Port Said, all the way home, the language of the ship's traffic was English... That, it

seems to me, is a bigger fact than the British Empire.

–Thompson, A.M., *Japan for a Week: Britain for Ever* (1910)

Thompson was right. The British Empire has been superseded by the even wider empire of English.

Soon after World War II there came an ever-increasing world-wide demand for English language studies. The 1960s saw the establishment of ELT as a profession. The University of London Institute of Education had launched a course for teachers of EFL back in 1932, but now came the beginning of specialist teacher-training courses in a succession of universities, including our own employer, the University of Manchester. In the period during which we were involved in EFL teaching, English came to be an ever more valuable international medium, providing millions with access to scientific, technical, medical and political information. By 1980 more than two-thirds of the world's scientists were publishing their work in the language, and 80% of all electronically stored information was in it. English had also become the language of international business, so it is hardly surprising that today the number of speakers of English as a second language has overtaken that of native-English speakers – roughly 350 million – and that users of English as a *foreign* language may number as many as a billion.

The global thirst for English created opportunities for teaching the language in a variety of cultures and in conditions that were often very demanding. Michael West's book *Teaching English in Difficult Circumstances*, which appeared in 1960, was based on many years' experience, mainly in Bengal. He was familiar with 'unfavourable circumstances' that included, among other things,

> A class consisting of over 30 pupils (more usually 40 or even 50), congested on benches... accommodated in an unsuitably shaped room, ill-graded, with a teacher who perhaps does not speak English very well or very fluently, working in a hot climate...

We too have worked in such circumstances; but whereas West concentrated on the classroom, we have moved outside it in recording these episodes in our careers.

In this little book we have written about such things as modes of travel, language, food, weather, places, personalities and wildlife. Sometimes exotic customs or conventions giving rise to humorous situations presented us with various challenges; sometimes there were tense political situations and uprisings that were far from funny. Stimulated by his own travels in post-Napoleonic Europe, Byron observed in *Don Juan*: "Tis strange – but true; for truth is always strange;/Stranger than fiction..." Our own experiences, in territories as far apart as Finland and Burma, may not have been stranger than fiction; but they did sometimes feel just as strange.

The title we have chosen echoes Compton Mackenzie's *All Over the Place* (1948). In the process of gathering material for a history of the Indian war effort, Mackenzie had completed a massive itinerary that included Burma and Nepal, countries where we too have worked and in which we maintain a strong interest. His subtitle was *Fifty thousand miles by sea, air, road and rail*; and it is simply because our own ELT careers also spanned many thousands of miles and took us to thirty countries – and not because of our students' poor command of the language! – that we have added the word *English* to Mackenzie's title.

We hope that the following episodes will give the reader some idea of what it felt like to operate far and wide as an 'ELT man' throughout the three decades from 1960 to 1990. The book falls into two halves: Gerry's contributions, then Bob's. The episodes in each half are in chronological order but can be read in any order. We have changed a few names here and there so as to protect certain individuals from possible embarrassment or repercussions, but all the places described are real and all the events actually happened.

– GWA & RRJ, September 2000

ACKNOWLEDGEMENTS

We are indebted to The British Council for giving us the opportunity to work in most of the countries that feature in this book. We also owe special thanks to the University of Manchester, our employer for much of the period covered in our episodes, for enabling us to pursue work in other countries. We want to thank the many people in those countries who made us welcome, extended their kind hospitality and cooperated so helpfully. In addition, we are grateful to Dr Stoddard Martin for the patience and editorial skills he has shown throughout the compilation and publication of this book.

Bob also wishes to express his thanks to Jim Burns for some early suggestions concerning the book; to Ulf and Marjatta Roos for information on Finnish words for snow conditions and ski tracks; to Alan Matthews for the arrangements he made in Portugal; to Jane Jordan for her useful suggestions and advice; and to Khin Thant Han for her help in putting his episodes on disc.

Gerry Abbott's three Burma episodes are abridged and revised extracts from his book *Back to Mandalay* (London: Impact, 1990). Quotations in Bob Jordan's episode 'On Top of the World' are from Edmund Hillary's book *Schoolhouse in the Clouds* (Hodder and Stoughton, London, 1964).

Part I:
Gerry Abbott

When I was six I got shifted out of London's East End because of the blitz, leaving the grey streets of Bow for the primroses and bluebells of Shamley Green, a village in the depths of Surrey. My life as an evacuee being rather nomadic, I attended six primary schools before taking and passing the new eleven-plus exam and finding myself in King Edward VI Royal Grammar School, Guildford. Here I failed Geography and History, Physics and Chemistry, and (most dismally) Maths every year, so when the new 'O' Level exams approached I was shunted into the class of no-hopers, Upper Four X. I was still entered for eight subjects, but in school time I was from now on encouraged to spend most of my hours sketching Guildford's riverside and High Street because I was good at Art, the one subject I was expected to pass with flying colours. Most evenings I spent fishing in the River Wey and wondering what was to become of me when I left school. When I unexpectedly passed all but Maths and History the Headmaster persuaded my parents, who had hoped I'd get out to work and bring some money in, to agree to my staying on.

For truancy I'd often been given 'six of the best', and for refusing to join the Combined Cadet Force or the Scouts because my parents couldn't afford the clothing and equipment I'd need, I had been put into a small group of misfits called 'The Squash Mob'. While others were out playing soldiers or pitching tents, I spent every Friday afternoon doing things like polishing the library floor or sweeping the quadrangle and passageways.

Nevertheless I got four 'A' Levels, left school, went into the Army to do my National Service, was commissioned and went back to my school to flaunt myself in my 2nd Lieutenant's uniform in front of the master in charge of the Cadets. Then, having gone to University College, London, I found a girlfriend, attended numerous parties, demonstrated in Parliament fields in favour of going into Hungary to stop the Soviet tanks ("Gimme a rifle!" I yelled) and shouted against the invasion of Suez. Somehow I obtained an Honours Degree in English.

I decided to train as a teacher of English as a foreign language. ("*Foreign* language?" my friends objected, "but it's *not* a foreign language!") I then discovered that neither the Ministry of Education nor my local education authority would give a grant to a teacher trainee who, on qualifying, would probably go and teach somewhere far more sunny. I therefore borrowed from the couple who employed my mother as a servant the sum (princely in 1958) of £300; this, along with vacation earnings, got me through the year's training. And this, to coin a phrase, is where the story really starts.

That loan did the trick. I'd no sooner qualified as a teacher specialising in the teaching of English as a foreign language than The British Council offered both me and my fiancée posts in Bangkok, and we felt financially secure enough to get married. At that time almost all Council staff were drawn from Oxford or Cambridge, so on my application form I had proudly listed London University and recorded my place of birth as 'Bow, E3' rather than just 'London'. I was told that shortly before my wife and I arrived in Bangkok in 1959 the British Council's Representative there had looked up from the advance papers with astonishment and exclaimed to his staff,

"Good Lord! They're sending us an educated Cockney!"

1: "Mekong!"

As soon as I could, I set about earning a little extra so as to be able to pay the money back to my mother's employer within one year, as I had promised. It was for this purpose alone that I started giving evening classes in Mr Sanoe's private school in Thonburi, just across the river from Bangkok proper. It was there one evening that I bumped into Mr Roberts in a corridor on his way to a class. He was carrying a pile of Eckersley's *Essential English for Foreign Students*; as he tucked them under his left arm and we shook hands, I noticed that he was grubby and unshaven and that his voice was slurred. When he started making disparaging remarks about the Thais, I hastily excused myself and hurried off to my class. Thereafter I always used the steps at the other end of the corridor to avoid meeting him.

"Mekong!"

As the singing died down and the red-white-and-blue striped national flag began to rise limply up the mast on a still, humid morning that was already uncomfortably warm, I thought I must have imagined that cry for help. It cannot have been much more than a hoarse whisper, for as I looked around I saw no sign that anyone else had heard. The children, dressed in neat navy-blue and white school uniforms, were drawn up in columns like naval cadets on a passing-out parade. Having just finished chanting the national anthem, they stood to attention to watch the jerky progress of the flag. Then, in the silence, everyone heard the agonised cry again:

"Mekong!"

The upturned faces of the children swivelled away from the flag towards the far end of the school building. It was a U-shaped three-storey concrete block whose wings embraced the playground on which the youngsters were now drawn up, class by class. Leaning over the railing on the second floor balcony was a figure that drew a collective gasp from the watchers below.

It was Mr Roberts, and he was naked.

I took a step backwards and stood next to Mr Sanoe. I had learned to say his name so that it ended with a rising tone and therefore sounded like someone asking, "Sir Nir?". As owner of a private school in Thonburi, he was quite prosperous and therefore fairly – well, let us be kind and say *portly*. People said that, for a male Thai, he was unusually energetic. When on foot he certainly went about his business at a very rapid waddle; and he certainly had his podgy fingers in various other pies, some just across the river in Bangkok and some down south, near

Malaya. Equally certainly he preferred to undertake even the shortest of trips in an ancient Chevrolet, a huge battered limousine which (I knew from bitter experience) was only just large enough to accommodate his driver, himself, his even more portly wife, their seven children and me.

He undertook no work that he could pass on to others. I realised immediately that I had been a fool to step back and join him, but at the same time I couldn't help feeling sorry for the fellow in his present predicament. His heavy round face, close to my right shoulder, would at the best of times shine like fresh putty, but that faint sheen had now broken out into beads of sweat and his shirt was turning transparent. For a few seconds we stood looking up at the apparition on the second floor, which was again calling for a bottle of Mekong.

Mr Roberts had until recently run a rubber plantation somewhere down in Malaya, but as independence approached he had been persuaded to give way to a local manager. The loneliness and boredom of plantation management had made both *Tuan* Roberts and his wife more and more dependent on the comforts of sundowner gins and postprandial whiskies. They had enjoyed a lifestyle which, when they moved northwards into Thailand, their meagre savings could no longer provide. Gin and whisky being far too expensive they now made do with the cheap local spirit; and since there was no other job that they could hold down, they were doing what the down-and-out Englishman abroad usually ended up doing – teaching English in a private school.

I was teaching in the same school to be sure, but there were significant differences. Newly-arrived in the East and just twenty-four, I was qualified to teach English and Mr Roberts not; I had a full-time job and was doing extra teaching here solely in order to pay back a loan, whereas he had no other employment; I had a house to live in, and Roberts and his wife had only a tiny room at the end of that corridor up there. And *I* had a work permit.

Mr Sanoe had been worried about this last legal nicety when taking on the Robertses but had hitherto been willing to take the risk of employing both of them. Now as he began to wipe his neck with a large white handkerchief, I could see by the mixture of horror and disgust on his usually impassive face that things were going to change.

A controlled hubbub had broken out, the boys chattering excitedly and the girls stifling giggles with hands over their mouths. Then the school janitor in his khaki uniform came striding along the balcony and shepherded the pale naked figure through a door and out of sight. Mr Sanoe turned to a teacher standing on his right and issued some brief commands, whereupon the shocked teachers began leading the smirking children away form by form. He then turned to me.

"Ah. Mister Abort. Mister Lobert not good for my nice plivate sakoon. Not good for Police to come here. Not good for sakoon. He dring too much. Missus Lobert too. I try to talk to him but he don' risten. You are Engrish. I lather plefer *you* tell him he must go. You – "

I was trying to picture myself, a raw newcomer, squaring up to a drunken Mr Roberts; I didn't like the idea one bit. When I imagined myself talking like a Dutch uncle to a temporarily sober Mr Roberts, a man older than my father, I liked the idea even less. Normally I taught here only on Tuesday and Thursday evenings. Why did this have to happen on the one and only morning when I was present, having volunteered to stand in for an absent teacher? No, I couldn't do it.

"Mr Sanoe, it is a very nice school. And it is a great pity that this has happened. But Mr and Mrs Roberts don't work for me, they work for you. *You* must tell them to go. And if they don't go, you will *have* to bring in the Police."

"But I tell him before, must not dring so much or I fire him. He not risten to me. He risten to you."

It was time to go and teach.

"I'm sorry," I said. "I must go."

The following Tuesday evening I found Mrs Roberts, whom I had seen from a distance but not met, coming towards me in the corridor. She was cuddling a pile of Eckersleys and walking in that over-erect and over-careful way that heavy drinkers have. She greeted me in a haughty distant way as if I were a coolie and passed by me, leaving behind a heavy whiff of scent and an even more powerful smell of spirits.

Things came to a head on the Thursday. Night was falling as I arrived. Mr Sanoe was waiting for me by my classroom door, sweating and fretting. Neither of the Robertses had shown up for their classes that day. They had refused to come out of their room, which was locked.

Please could I –

I said I would first teach my two classes and then try to help. The thought of having to deal with the pair of them spoiled the lessons, after which I reluctantly went to their room at the end of the dark corridor, asking Mr Sanoe to wait out of sight on the stairs, and knocked on the door. There was a short, gruff response that I did not understand.

"Mr Roberts? It's only me. Gerry."

I put my ear to the door. There was another grunt and a series of rustling noises, followed by a lengthy fumbling with keys and lock. Finally the door opened a little and one bleary eye stared blankly at me. Mr Roberts put his head out and looked left and right as I spoke.

"Look, I'm afraid Mr Sanoe's had enough. He's very angry and he'll have to fetch the Police if you haven't left by – "

"C'mere. Siddown a minute."

A large hand gripped my upper arm, yanked me into the unlit room, thrust me on to a single bed and closed the door. As he turned the key in the lock, Roberts began to plead, and as he was speaking, my eyes became accustomed to the dimness. What light there was came through a small window from an exterior lamp. On a bed in the opposite corner lay the still, silent figure of Mrs Roberts, half-naked and apparently asleep. There were empty bottles on a small table and on the floor; the room stank of sweat and liquor. He was sitting next to me on his rumpled dank bed, wheedling and whining.

"Look, you're not a bloody wog you're Brish'n we Brish gotta stick toge – together, 'n that right? You wouldn' wanna see me an' the Mem chucked out? Don' want us in Malaya, don' want us here… Have a word with ol' wossname. He'll listen to you. We Brish gotta – "

"Listen, I've already had a word with him," I lied as he began sniffing.

He raised his head and turned to face me as I continued.

"But it's no good, he won't listen. He's determined to have the Police cart you off before evening classes start tomorrow, and I wouldn't want to be in one of *their* jails. If I were you I'd collect my pay while the going's good and go to the Embassy as soon as you can tomorrow."

Many people might say he deserved no sympathy, but I felt like a heel. I was also out of my depth in this sort of situation. As he turned to the low table to get himself a drink, I took my chance and made for the door. I twisted the key and the handle and yanked it open; Mr Sanoe stepped back to the top of the stairs. He had of course been listening. Pretending that I had only now noticed him coming upstairs, I called out down the echoing staircase, with Mr Roberts now clutching at my back.

"Ah! Mr Sanoe! By four o'clock, did you say?"

"Uh? Oh, collect. By four. If not, Police come to ask for work permit."

The hand released its grip and the door slammed shut behind me. I drove home still feeling vaguely ashamed; I think Mr Sanoe felt the same way, for he never again mentioned the Robertses. The following Tuesday evening I went to my classroom via the far end of the corridor as usual and taught my two classes. There was no sign of the Robertses, so I plucked up courage and walked along to the little room at the near end of the corridor. It was not locked. When I opened the door, there was a smell of disinfectant. I called out; and when there was no answer, I reached in and flicked on the light. The room was now what it presumably had been before the Robertses arrived: a store-cupboard.

2: THE CAVES OF PETCHABURI

I locked my legs around the vertical bamboo pole and, clutching it with my right hand, leaned to my left to look inside the rusty metal container lashed to the middle of the crossbar. There, sitting on a nest of criss-crossed bones in the blazing sunlight, was a human skull. I pulled myself upright and held on with both hands, for a few moments at a loss for words. Sweat was tickling my forehead. Nick called impatiently from below.

"Well? What's in it?"

"A skeleton."

"You're kidding."

Holding on tight, I leaned over again and stretched out my left hand until the spread fingers closed over the bone. When I lifted the skull, the lower jaw stayed in the nest.

"Look."

Nick squinted up but said nothing.

Replacing the skull gently, I slithered back down one of the angled bamboo struts that propped up the vertical posts.

"What do you make of that then, Nick?"

"Bloody sight more interesting than caves."

On that day in 1960 Nick and I, both of us teachers of English in Bangkok, were having a day off. He taught in a prestigious secondary school, I in the adjacent Patumwan teacher-training college and its attached demonstration school. The short cool season was over and the rains (apart from the usual 'mango showers') still a long way off. For this public holiday, several teachers from each institution – all of them women – had hired a bus to take them to the Khao Luang caves near Petchaburi, about a hundred miles to the south. Would we like to come along? It would be sanook, they said, enjoyable – sanook mahk-mahk, very very enjoyable. Nick didn't seem too keen on the idea, but I was interested. For the sake of solidarity, he came along.

When we arrived as arranged at the point of departure on Patumwan campus at eight, the sky was a cloudless blue and already it was hot. A dilapidated bus was waiting under the large rain-tree that stood outside the college staff-room, but there wasn't a soul in sight. By nine, the dozen or so other teachers had arrived in ones and twos. Another ten minutes passed before the driver came into view, flip-flopping across the dusty compound and finishing off a snack wrapped in a banana-leaf. Licking his fingers and sliding into the driver's seat, he kicked off his flip-flops and turned to greet us with a broad grin.

"Sawatdee, khrap!"

"Sawatdee, kha," chorused the smiling ladies.

"At bloody last," muttered an unsmiling Nick.

The roads outside Bangkok were narrow, steeply-cambered and pot-holed, and the tarmac on either side had a habit of crumbling and cracking off, leaving sharp and pitted verges. The lorry drivers drove as if there was no tomorrow; whenever a truck came hurtling towards us with headlights blazing, the bus would lean over at an alarming angle with its tyres thumping along those edges, high above a klong (canal) or paddy field. As we rumbled and bounced southwards, Nick confessed that he couldn't stand caves. He didn't just dislike them, he actually sweated at the thought of going inside one. Being about ten years older than I was, he had joined the army, fought in Burma and been awarded the Military Cross. I found it strange that courage and claustrophobia could go hand in hand but didn't pursue the matter.

When the bus finally swayed to a halt in a cloud of blinding dust, we all descended and set off towards a rocky outcrop at the foot of which gaped the wide, dark mouth of a cave with Buddha images gleaming just inside like gold teeth. Looking uneasy and pale, Nick stopped at the entrance, telling the teachers that he was just going to get something to eat at a nearby food-stall, and I went in. In the dim coolness, I admired the stalactites and stalagmites that had been growing towards each other through the centuries and gazed at the glowing Buddha images smiling at each other through the dark. Beneath these eternal smiles, my Thai colleagues chatted softly to each other and bent at their individual devotions. Out in the sun again, with my eyes screwed up against the light and my skin once again prickling in the heat, I bought a snack and shared with Nick a bottle of cold Beer Singha bought from a vendor. He didn't ask what I'd seen in the cave.

When it was time to leave, the driver didn't take the route that we had come by but turned along a narrow and rutted track. We swished along for a while between trees and bamboos and then came out into open country – dry paddy-fields and scrub, islanded with great stands of bamboo and sudden outcrops of rock that looked like small crumbling volcanoes. For what seemed like hours, the bus rumbled on slowly in the afternoon heat, raising behind it a screen of dust as bright as a vapour trail. Then in the middle of nowhere the engine hiccuped, and we jolted to a halt, everyone coughing as the hot, overtaking dust poured in through the open windows. Tumbling out into the sunlight and dusting themselves down, the teachers remonstrated with the driver. The fuel tank was empty, he said, but a mile or two ahead there was a place where he thought he could scrounge some petrol. We got the impression that he had underestimated either the length of this 'short-cut' or the amount of fuel the bus would use up when travelling on a bad track in low gear. We stood watching as he flip-flopped away down the track with his jerrycan.

All the ladies climbed back into the bus so as to avoid darkening their complexions and were soon sweating in their solar-powered oven. Nick and I preferred to go for a stroll. If we weren't back by the time the driver returned, we said, they should tell him to give us a blast on his horn. We walked ahead a few dozen yards, then turned left towards an outcrop of rock that resembled a miniature Vesuvius. At the foot of this there was a nice clump of bamboo where we could sit in the shade. It was here that we came upon that strange, disturbing scene and the canned skeleton.

What we noticed first was a rectangle of recently-dug earth. Nearby were the ashes of a small fire, and just beyond stood a strange bamboo construction very like a half-sized rugby football goalpost except that, in the middle of the H-shaped framework, there was another vertical pole. Each of the outer posts was buttressed by three bamboo struts lashed to the posts at head height, and tied low on the right-hand post was a rusty old tin can half full of burned-out joss-sticks. The 'goal' was about four yards wide and three high, and the 'grave' large enough to accommodate an adult; but what intrigued us most was the rusty, square-based canister up there, lashed to the intersection of the crossbar and the central vertical post. What, if anything, did that contain? So I climbed up and looked.

I agreed with Nick: this scene was far more interesting than the caves. As he had been in Thailand a year or so before I arrived, I thought he might be able to explain the significance of it.

"What do these things mean? What's it all for?"

"Damned if I know."

As I walked round the 'goalposts', he went to look at the freshly dug earth, stirred the nearby ashes with his foot and then, crouching by the 'grave', looked up.

"Some weird sect, perhaps?" he suggested.

"Practising sacrifices, you mean? No. Too open, too near the track. It could be just Communist scare tactics. What d'you think?"

"I doubt it. This is too far north for them. They're down by the Malayan border."

"I'll go and ask the others," I said, my curiosity aroused.

When I reached the bus and excitedly told our lady colleagues what we had found, their hands stopped fanning, their eyes widened and their lips tightened. It was nothing, nothing, they said. Leave it alone. So I returned to Nick.

We stood discussing possibilities for some minutes. It was only when we went to sit down in the shade of the bamboo thicket that I looked past the strange framework and saw it was not a goal but a gateway. Beyond it, the dry low scrub had been roughly hacked down to make a narrow stubbly path that ran straight up the rocky hillside. Scrambling, up with Nick following, I found the path getting steeper and steeper. Then suddenly it levelled out and I pitched forward towards darkness. My heart pounded. The path had become a sort of ledge; being on all fours, I was gripping the threshold of a black pit, a yawning cavern. I had almost fallen to my death in the bowels of the hill. Below me and all around there was only cool blackness, except that some distance ahead, now that my eyes were becoming accustomed to the gloom, I could see a narrow chink of daylight. The sudden realisation that the hill was a hollow shell added to my sense of insecurity.

As I backed away, I imagined the ledge collapsing and the hill swallowing me. Nick's head appeared above the ledge.

"Slow right down, Nick, and don't come too close."

He saw the black hole, rolled away from it and sat puffing and panting. Then he pointed.

"What the hell's that thing sticking out of it?"

I turned to look. In my panic I hadn't noticed that from the left side of this black hole there emerged, almost vertically out of the darkness, a stout bamboo into which a pair of sturdy pegs of wood had been fitted. Leaning across and peering down over the edge until my eyes adjusted themselves again, I saw that more pegs were driven in on alternate sides; I could just see that a further length with similar rungs had been lashed to the first, continuing the descent into the black depths.

"Sort of ladder," I reported. "Seems to go a long way down, too."

"Try dropping a stone in."

I let a small piece of rock fall over. After a long time we heard a faint hollow thud, but neither of us could remember the formula for estimating how far down the cave floor was. Nevertheless, I tried again.

This time we heard a loud clang. All we had found out was that it was a very long way to the bottom and that someone had left behind down there a large metal object, probably a container. I was very curious but knew Nick would never go down there, and I certainly wouldn't go alone. So that was that. We sat back and puzzled: if not a Communist den, then what?

The bus horn blared.

As we scrambled down, we were still casting about for an explanation. I was now arguing that the cave was the home of a colony of swiftlets, the species whose valuable nests were gathered annually for the making of bird's nest soup. The gatherers were expert at making bamboo scaffolding – I had seen this much in a film – and the cave was silent now because it wasn't the nesting season. The metal container might be for the nest-gatherers' drinking-water. Their trade was very lucrative, so they might go to great lengths to scare away intruders – hence the bamboo gateway with the skull. As for the grave-like patch of earth, well, they might even kill to protect their trade. But it didn't sound very likely.

As we approached the bus, we decided to note the route back to the main road so that we could return with two British friends who had rock-climbing experience and the right equipment for exploring the cave. Back in the bus, we told the teachers no more about what we had found; and the very fact that they clearly didn't want to know deepened the mystery. Nick made notes about the route as far as the main road; then we sat back and chatted about other things. At some point in a conversation about our school days, Nick mentioned that he'd loved exploring caves when he was a kid. I puzzled over that as the strips of golden sky reflected in the roadside klong darkened and the open fields gave way to the teak-and-bamboo suburbs of Thonburi.

We were back at work in Bangkok, and the weeks had gone by. Neither of us had found anyone able, or perhaps willing, to explain the significance of what we had seen. Following up my own theory, I had consulted various reference books, none of which conceded the presence of the swiftlet *Collocalia fuciphaga* in or anywhere near the Petchaburi area. Because our rock-climbing friends had left Bangkok, we never did mount the proposed expedition; but later on I think I did find the answer to the other question that had been puzzling me.

During one of his many boozy dinner-parties, Nick downed several beers too many, became morose, gathered an audience on the verandah, walked off down the short garden and ceremonially flung his Military Cross into the klong that slid inkily by, just a few feet away. On the verandah someone from the Embassy told me quietly how he had won the medal. While in action as a junior officer somewhere in Upper Burma, he had received a message that his only brother had been killed in a nearby skirmish. Nick's own platoon was at the time pinned down by fire from a concrete pillbox on the brow of a hill. On receiving the news, Nick had seen red. Charging up the slope alone and reaching the Japanese emplacement miraculously unharmed, he had lobbed a couple of grenades through the narrow embrasures.

The Embassy man stopped Nick as he came weaving back across the lawn and climbed the verandah steps. He told Nick that he knew about his MC and how he'd earned it and asked him why on earth he had thrown the medal away. Nick turned, screwed up his eyes and looked out into the darkness, seeing some horror there.

"*You* didn't see the poor buggers trapped inside," he muttered.

Three dozen years later the whole episode was beginning to fade in my memory when I came across a possible explanation for the ladder into the cavern. It was a 'News in Brief' item in *The Guardian* of 6 March 1998:

Killed for dung

Five men died in eastern Thailand at the weekend when an unknown assailant threw a grenade into their midst as they collected prized bat dung, which is used to make organic fertiliser.

The fact that the bat dung was valuable enough to kill for in this instance might explain the presence of that canned skeleton on the crossbar all those years ago. Then again, it might not.

3: Two Bridges

"China? Out of the question," snapped the British Council Representative.

It was 1962. As a resident English teacher working for the Thai Ministry of Education, I had been planning to take advantage of the fact that through the good offices of the Embassy of Indonesia, a country that maintained diplomatic relations with what was known at the time as 'Red China', I could fly to Peking (as it was then known) and see a city generally out of bounds to westerners. However, the British Embassy must have discovered my plan and informed the Council, under whom I was working on contract, that I was in danger of becoming another 'Red under the bed' at a time when the phrase 'better dead than Red' was the slogan of the Western Alliance. When obstacles were put in my way, I decided instead to drive my little grey Morris Minor over the Cambodian border in order to see Angkor Wat; but by now the *Bangkok Post* was reporting details about the severing of relations between Thailand and her neighbour. Diplomatic tensions recurred quite regularly because of a standing dispute over Khao Phra Viharn, a venerable hilltop temple complex that straddled the common border, but this time the situation looked serious. Still, I was determined to go.

"Cambodia, indeed! Certainly not," said the Rep.

When I made further official enquiries, I was told that as things were going there could well be war and the border would be closed; but when I asked expatriate old-timers who had no connection with the Embassy or the Council, I gathered that a teacher such as myself would have no problem in getting to see Nakorn Wat, as the Thai called Angkor. I have forgotten the tiresome details concerning the obstacles put in my way by British officialdom, but two obstacles on the journey itself I remember very clearly. They had no business being obstacles, because they were both bridges.

Having decided to go ahead, I needed only to drive down to New Road and walk up and down among the many kiosks selling various currencies to discover that, because of the hostility between the two governments, I could buy Cambodian money at a rate of exchange vastly more favourable than usual. After bargaining with two or three of these dealers, I came away with so many thick wads of grubby Cambodian notes that I had to stuff some of them inside my shirt until I got back to the car.

My wife and I had promised to take with us two other English teachers, Peter and Sam. The monsoon was over, the day of our departure broke cool and bright, and the sun was still low when we picked up our two friends. I drove to the Victory Monument (*what* victory, for goodness sake?) and turned north on to the airport road, a narrow thoroughfare lined with rain-trees and bordered on each side by a sluggish inky klong. As it was early, people were still squatting beside or standing in these canals, some washing or cleaning their teeth, others relieving themselves. Soon we had left Don Muang airport behind and were into open country, the little grey Morris purring along on a straight and narrow metalled road raised several feet above the bare paddy-fields. The canvas canopy was folded down, the low sun was on our faces, a cool breeze was in our hair and we were making good time.

Then I noticed that a short way ahead the road, one that I knew well, seemed to come to a sudden end.

Stopping the car where the tarmac ended, I got out to inspect the boulders and rubble that confronted us, stretching ahead for as far as the eye could see. Looking to the right, we could see what had happened: the monsoon flooding, sweeping in from the left, had lifted off the surface in large sheets, depositing the road-metal in the fields; the waters had then washed away all but the largest rocks forming the road's foundation. The paddy-fields to our right were littered with great black scabs of tarmac, and the highway looked like the remains of an old castle wall. We set off again, very slowly. My trusty Morris Minor crawled and bumped and meandered without complaint. For mile after mile the little car negotiated the rocks, my passengers getting out in the worst places both to lighten the load and to act as guides, until at last the tarmac appeared in its proper place. We sped on to the junction south of Ayuthaya, where it was necessary to turn eastwards towards Cambodia along a road that was new to me.

I had planned to arrive at Siam Reap, the little town near Angkor Wat, by sunset; but already the sun was high, the canvas roof back in place over our heads. We had lost a lot of time, so although the road was only just wide enough for two cars to pass I put my foot down hard on this eastward run. Twice we might have had a serious accident: once we just missed a water-buffalo that appeared out of some undergrowth and lumbered slowly across our path; later we rounded a bend to find two vultures hunched over some dead creature lying in the middle of the road. One bird flew off immediately, but the other must have been gorged: it raised its bloodsoaked head, did several knees-bends and flapped mightily as the Morris continued to rush towards it, despite my frantic efforts with the brakes. As we were about to hit the thing, its leg and wing muscles at last managed to lift it off the road, and I ducked as it hurtled towards the windscreen. For a moment its wide black wings blotted out the view, its legs swinging beneath its bulging body. As we rushed underneath it, I heard a claw scrape over the canvas above my head.

It was mid-afternoon, windless and very hot when we pulled in at the dusty little border town of Aranya Prathet and tried to find an official who could stamp our passports. I remember driving from office to office, each raised wooden building sporting a limp Thai flag and apparently inhabited by just one sleepy officer. Each successive officer very pleasantly indicated that he was not able to deal with our problem, and it became clear that no-one wished to take the responsibility for sending us into enemy territory. In the end I asked some local people where the border was; they pointed along a track, and we found ourselves pulling up at one of those counterbalanced poles that are painted white and forbid you to proceed. A few yards beyond it stood a small plank bridge that had stout handrails on either side and was wide enough to take only one vehicle at a time. It spanned a deep dried-up ditch, the border. I switched off the engine and got out. No-one appeared. A wooden shack nearby was empty and my shouts went unheard. The others climbed out of the car and stood in the thin shade of a small tree. We waited.

And waited.

So near and yet so far. In the end, the temptation was too great. I went to the barrier, lifted it and waited again, expecting someone nearby to shout 'Halt!' in Thai, or someone a few yards away on the other side of the ditch to scream the equivalent in Khmer. When nothing happened, I got into the car and drove very slowly across the plank bridge, hoping that this was not the sort of offence for which one could be shot in the back by a Thai border guard or in the chest by a Cambodian one. Still nothing happened, so I called the others across and we drove into no-man's-land. After half a mile or so, we came across an apparently deserted compound of bare earth with a flagpole and three low wooden buildings. This was clearly the Cambodian border post, so I stopped and called out again. Once again there was no answer, so I climbed out, went up to an open door, walked in and almost jumped out of my skin when a face appeared, very close to my own, above the narrow counter inside. I don't know who was more startled, the sleepy Cambodian or the sheepish Englishman.

Once we had finished grinning with embarrassment, I explained in bits of French and English that I worked for the British Council (which in both languages can be made to sound very much like the British Consulate) and that my colleagues were waiting outside. The friendly fellow saw no problem. He obligingly stamped our passports and wished us *bon voyage*, and in no time we were on our way to Angkor Wat with the sun setting behind us. By the time we arrived at Siam Reap, my friend Peter, who had travelled in the seat behind mine, declared that the back seat springs no longer deserved the name (which was true) and that he had a shattered coccyx and dislocated spine (which I doubted but had no way of disproving). We found a grubby, paint-peeled hotel, retired immediately and got up early. Glued into our breakfast omelette was a quick-fried cockroach, I remember, but it was good to have fresh bread and coffee.

This may well be the only account ever written of a trip to Angkor which gives no description of that stunning complex of colossal blocks of stone raised and carved by almost superhuman effort and then in many places, slowly riven and tumbled by the seemingly minuscule powers of seeds and rootlets. To do it justice, I would have to write a book; in any case, the scene has been well described and photographed many times before. Having marvelled over it for a couple of days, we decided to continue to Pnom Penh, checked out of our little hotel in Siam Reap and headed south-eastwards.

About halfway to the capital, we reached the township of Kompong Thom. Here the wooden steps and stilts of all the houses had intriguingly been painted a bright pale blue, the sort of colour that might be associated by older readers with the name Reckitt and by younger ones with swimming pools. We debated stopping for a beer and a bite, but decided to press on. This turned out to be a fortunate decision because, when we reached Pnom Penh, we were told that the little town we had passed through was a plague area: the blue stuff contained a poison specifically intended to kill the rats that were spreading the disease. If we had stopped in the area and it had become known to the authorities, we would have been held in isolation for a considerable time. As it was, we were free to spend a couple of nights in Pnom Penh, a city proclaimed as at least half French by its tree-lined avenues, its open-air cafés, its fresh crispy bread and its wines.

I timed our return journey so as to ensure that we wouldn't need to stop for food anywhere near the plague area, and we spent the night in the same little hotel in Siam Reap. On leaving the following morning, we expected no trouble at the Cambodian border post – after all, we had valid entry visas – but we did wonder what would happen at the bridge on the far side of no-man's-land. In the event, although we were stopped there by Thai immigration officers, our presence was explained by their conclusion that we had never left the country. The fact that we had just driven back across the little wooden bridge and had a Cambodian stamp in our passports was as nothing compared to the fact that there was no exit visa. There was no exit visa, therefore we had not left Thailand, therefore the barrier could be raised and we were free to proceed. Thus far, then, the return journey had gone very smoothly and we set off westwards in high spirits. It was a Thai road sign, one that in our hurry we had not seen when we passed this way before, that set us heading towards our second, and far more formidable, obstacle-bridge.

The sign proclaimed that here was the beginning of a grand new highway to Bangkok. The makeshift arrow pointing to the left along a dirt track held out the promise of a painless homeward trip, not along the two sides of a triangle that we had followed on the outward journey, but straight to Bangkok along its hypotenuse. We had stopped, and there was some indecision. As I had done all the driving and was beginning to find the trip wearisome, I decided to follow the new track. After a few miles it became clear that the 'beginning' of the highway referred not to its starting-point but to its stage of construction. For half an hour or more we sped towards the low sun along a dirt foundation raised high above the surrounding paddy-fields. This highway was admittedly wide, but the soil was deeply furrowed by the wheels of bullock-carts, and we raised a thick curtain of copper-coloured dust. I slowed down as we approached a band of brightness that we had seen in the distance and which now lay across our path. When we came to a halt, a thick red cloud overtook us, and in the choking dust we had to keep our faces covered for a minute or so.

In the settling haze we got out and walked forward to inspect the problem. Across our path, its surface about four metres below us, lay a wide klong. Its sluggish yellow waters barely moved. True, there was a timber bridge across it, but either it had been abandoned or (more likely) was still in a rudimentary stage of construction, for it had no floor and no sides. From above, this skeleton would have looked like a huge capital H consisting of five logs thrown across the gap; from down in the klong itself you would have seen that the framework was supported by a pair of log pillars at each bank and in the middle. To cap it all, the two horizontal logs at this end did not quite match up to the two at the other end, so that even if the front wheels of the Morris were the right distance apart, they would have to shimmy to the right a little when they reached the middle of the bridge. Peter and Sam shook their heads and looked at me reproachfully, as if I were the engineer responsible for this contraption.

A closer inspection yielded two encouraging pieces of information: the wheels *were* the right distance apart, and the (almost) parallel logs had been roughly flattened and were about a foot wide – considerably wider than the tyres. The span of the bridge (at least twelve yards) was daunting, but we had come a long way down this new super-highway and already the sun was setting. In the hope that there would be no more bridges as rudimentary as this one, I decided to go ahead. I got Peter and Sam to walk across with two suitcases each; they would be able to watch the front wheels and give signals. Of the two evils, walking or being a passenger, my wife opted for the latter. I started the engine. When we stopped at the very edge, I had terrible visions of my little Morris slipping between the logs and plunging into the thick yellow water, visions that prompted me to put down the canvas roof.

As I let out the clutch and the car inched its way forward, Peter and Sam beckoned me with slow upward movements of their forearms. There was a bump as the front wheels climbed on to the logs, then another as the rear wheels followed. If the car slipped now, it would plunge about twelve feet and sink into the thick muddy water. Peter and Sam raised their palms, giving me the halt sign. The front tyres had obviously reached the join in the middle, for now they were signalling that I should turn the steering wheel to my right. This I promptly did, but the consternation in their waving arms immediately told me that I had turned too far. Further little twitching movements put me back on course, and I gently let out the clutch again. A twitch to the left, a few more yards and we were over. I confessed my sense of elation, my friends their great relief, and my poor wife her nausea.

The rest of the journey, through the cool darkness, was humdrum. By midnight we were home.

In New Road a few days later, I got a huge pile of baht for my left-over wads of notes because by then the Thai and Cambodian governments had, speaking purely metaphorically of course, mended their bridges.

Postscript: Some months after I finished writing this account, I happened to read an Italian journalist's report of his experiences in various parts of Asia (Tiziano Terzani's *A Fortune-teller Told Me*, HarperCollins, 1997). He describes how he went by road to 'the Thai city of Aranya Prathet' and on the morning of 18 April 1975 'walked across the iron bridge that spans the frontier'. 'Towards sunset' he was allowed to leave Cambodia. 'Later that evening', he adds, he was in the Oriental Hotel in Bangkok. The words 'city', 'iron' and 'that evening' suggest how much had changed in just thirteen years.

4: Delivered by Hand

The elderly colonel at the Foreign Office obviously thought I was too young for this sort of mission. He reminded me that this was the first cultural link with Hungary since the beginning of the Cold War, then stressed how careful I should be in my behaviour and guarded in my speech once I arrived in Budapest. I must remember that behind the Iron Curtain all officials and guides would be Party members, so I would have to be very circumspect in their presence. The hotels and other public places would have hidden microphones, so I was to inspect my room and be suspicious of any unexplained fixtures. There must be no hitches of any kind – absolutely none, understood? He offered further bits of advice; the one thing he didn't tell me was what I should do if I received a secret message.

It had been early on a summer afternoon in 1963, soon after I had returned from my four-year uninterrupted stint in Thailand and was living in London, that someone in The British Council had telephoned to enquire in a lazy, casual sort of way whether I'd like a trip to Hungary. Well, yes I would, but why? Um, because we're planning to have a short course for teachers of English there. Oh, I see... starting when? When? Er, let's see... next Thursday. *Next Thursday? But it's already Friday afternoon!* Ah, but Thursday's only when you'd have to *leave*: the course itself doesn't start until the Monday, you see. A-A-And we *are* in a bit of a spot: so few qualified people around, you see, at this time of year. And we need two people, and we've only got one so far. And you're known to us, and better the devil you know and so forth.

I said I'd have to think about it and the cheery voice said of course, of course, old chap; but I was to ring back with a definite answer before five because naturally he wouldn't be in the office tomorrow, Saturday. After a discussion with my wife and some further thought, I rang back.

"Look, if you're *that* desperate I'll go," I said. "But – "

"Splendid!"

"But who's this other person, and when can we meet? And what about our visas?"

My colleague, he said, was to be a chap called Peter and he already had a visa, but he was now on holiday overseas somewhere or other. I was to drop my passport in at the Council's duty desk in Davies Street the following morning before eleven, whereupon a courier would deliver it to the Hungarian consular office before midday. I complied with this order and then spent a relaxed weekend at home; but on Monday morning came another command. Tomorrow morning I was to report to an address in King Charles Street. This was for the Foreign Office briefing by a Colonel somebody-or-other, the man who failed to foresee that I might be given a secret message.

Once the Colonel had finished with me, I wanted to get down to business; but I was unable to plan anything much on my own. It wasn't until I arrived at Heathrow airport on the Thursday that I at last met Peter, a somewhat older man than me. A harassed courier arrived with our return tickets and passports just half an hour before take-off.

By the time Peter and I stepped onto the Hungarian tarmac, we had sketched out an agreed two-week programme. In the airport at Budapest we were met and escorted by a short, heavily-built and grim-faced woman who had weathered at least forty hard winters, whose measurements seemed to be about 40-40-40 and whose right boot might well (I imagined) conceal a lethal retractable blade. Once deposited in an old-fashioned, high-ceilinged hotel room, I did a quick survey. There was nothing behind the two large pictures on the wall. There were two unexplained little grilles – one above the door and one near the washbasin in the opposite corner – but I was too tired to care.

Left alone the following morning, Peter and I were able to go out on the terrace and dawdle over the breakfast of croissants, morello cherry jam and coffee. I say '*the* breakfast' because throughout our stay in Budapest, even though we were later moved to a more modern hotel, breakfast was always the same. That first morning we compared notes: yes, Peter's room also had two unexplained grilles, so although we both felt we might be over-suspicious we agreed never to talk about our Hungarian colleagues or discuss anything politically sensitive while we were indoors. We also discussed our grim-faced guide. She had a German name; I suspected that she was an East German security officer, but for our own purposes we decided to call her just 'Comrade'.

That afternoon a car came and took us to the Ministry of Education, where we expected the exchange of greetings and well-wishing to be, as usual, outwardly warm and genuine but in reality formal and insincere. To our delight, after being enthusiastically welcomed and introduced to three Ministry men who were clearly buddies, the five of us chatted informally (though mainly about things prior to 1945, I noticed) and a bottle of apricot brandy was produced. The initial formal toasting gave way to "Cheers!" and "Down the hatch!" and a second bottle appeared. Jokes were told, the afternoon slipped away and we were all very merry. By the time the third bottle was opened, my eyes were feeling scratchy and my mouth dry and I looked meaningfully at Peter, who tactfully extricated us. We felt quite wobbly on the way down the stairs but had the impression that we had come through some kind of test with flying colours.

Although we did quite a lot of preparation over the weekend, we also found time to go to Margitsziget, an island in the middle of the Danube, between Buda and Pest. Here we enjoyed a bathe in the hot spring waters that bubble up into the island and, on Sunday evening, an open-air concert of csárdás and other Hungarian pieces played under the stars by a spirited string orchestra.

The first week of the course went well. On our second weekend Comrade took us on a day trip to the historic town of Eger. I had read about brainwashing and knew something about the power of persuasion, but it was on this little trip that I first came up against the plate-glass barrier that indoctrination can erect between people.

Eger is not all that far from Budapest, but that train journey seemed interminable, not only because the train went slowly and stopped at every opportunity but also because of the tedium of having to converse with Comrade. Peter and I had been getting on well together and liked to chat, but by a series of interruptions Comrade made it clear that Peter and I should address ourselves not to each other but to her. This was presumably in order to prevent our expressing sinister private meanings that might elude her. When we therefore contented ourselves with addressing polite questions to her, she was nonetheless suspicious of our enquiries and killed the conversation with answers such as "The question does not arise", "We do not have that problem", and so on; and when she interrogated us, she refused to accept that we were answering truthfully. At some point I mentioned my years at University College, London. She leaned forward aggressively.

"You studied at London University?"

"Yes, I – "

"Ha! Then you are rich."

"Me? Rich? No, I – "

"Of *course* you are rich," she hissed. "In capitalist countries only the rich can go to universities."

As someone born in a terraced house in Bow, a boy who had managed to climb the educational ladder without the benefit of wealth or privilege, I resented Comrade's assumption and felt my face flushing. Fortunately, however, I was also by now sufficiently amused by her doctrinaire pronouncements to be able to smile.

I briefly told her of my educational background. I told her how via the 'Eleven Plus' and passes at 'O' and 'A' levels I had earned a County Major Scholarship – a full one, because my parents were too poor to contribute to my upkeep – and that this, plus a little money earned during vacations, had seen me through the three undergraduate years. I could see, by the hard set of her mouth and the occasional half-sigh, half-snort, that she was giving no credence to my tale. When I finished, she actually told me so.

"OK," I said, breaking the rules by addressing my colleague. "Tell us about your own education, Peter."

Peter told a very similar story, except that he had gone to Oxford (Ha! said Comrade) and had studied a different subject. Comrade found our amateurish efforts at propaganda so transparently preposterous that she actually managed a sort of laugh. By the time the train arrived, we were able get only brief glimpses of Eger before it was time to leave. Our return journey passed in almost complete silence.

The course continued to go well in its second week, and it became clear to us that the sixty or so participants fell into three groups. A couple of dozen were great anglophiles and mobbed us in the corridors between sessions: we discovered that these were specialist teachers of English. A group similar in number were cooperative but somewhat reserved: these turned out to be non-specialist language teachers. The remaining dozen or so, who maintained an unsmiling distance, were almost certainly Party members – maybe some of them informers. It was during the mid-morning break on Wednesday, when Peter was surrounded by one talkative bunch and I by another, that I received the secret message.

My left hand held a cup of coffee and my right arm was hanging by my side as I began to answer a question put by one of the senior Hungarian officials. In mid-sentence I felt some fingers press a piece of paper, folded small, into my right hand and close my fingers over it. The Colonel's briefing must have had some effect because I was able, without turning, pausing or batting an eyelid in front of that official, to complete my answer while putting my right hand casually into my trouser pocket to deposit the message there.

We had by now been transferred to a new hotel fairly close to the institute used for the course. At midday we would walk back to it for lunch and, since there was nothing worth looking at in the shops, I would study the scars of the Hungarian uprising, for here and there the buildings themselves still told of the terrible street fighting that had taken place seven years earlier. The disfigurements were mostly well above eye level: there were bricked-in windows, pitted facades, jagged ledges, places where some decorative pieces of stonework or stucco were missing and lines of pockmarks made by light machine-guns. Every day I was reminded of the heart-breaking broadcasts picked up by the BBC, transmitted only minutes before the free Hungarian radio went dead; the repeated plea 'Help us... Help us' had been followed by the national anthem with its stark message 'This is where you live, and this is where you must die'. But that had been in 1956, when Western Europe had stood in awe of the Soviet tanks and Britain – in cahoots with France and Israel – had been embroiled in the Suez fiasco. No help had come, and the tanks had rolled in.

When lunchtime came and Peter and I were walking back to our hotel, I quietly told him what had happened. We agreed that we shouldn't look at the paper out there in the street and that when we were back in the hotel we would read it silently and make no spoken comment on it. Once we were in my hotel room, I unfolded the message.

I don't remember the wording exactly, but it read very much like this:

> PLEASE MEET US TONIGHT AT ABOUT 8 O'CLOCK. TAKE TRAM 'X' AND ALIGHT AT THE THIRD STOP. THERE TAKE BUS 'Y' AND GO TO THE TERMINUS. HERE STREET 'Z' GOES UP A HILL. THERE IS A HIGH WALL ON THE LEFT. WALK BESIDE IT AND WE WILL MEET YOU.

When we had each looked at it in silence, I opened a book at page 100 and slipped the message inside.

As we walked back after lunch, we discussed what we should do. The Colonel would certainly have said, "Do nothing." On the other hand, since no names were mentioned and no precise address was given, we doubted whether it could be a trap. If the Hungarian authorities had wanted to see us, they would simply have asked Comrade to bring us in; and the British Embassy would hardly need to resort to such stealth. No, the message must be from a group of participants – probably the anglophile set. But the question remained. Should we go? If we did, we might be followed or observed and perhaps get *them* into serious trouble, but if we didn't go we would certainly disappoint and perhaps offend them. We looked up at the scarred facades and blind windows and decided to go.

During the afternoon session I was on the lookout for any signals, spoken or otherwise, that might identify one or more of our prospective hosts; but by the end of the day we were none the wiser. We had no idea how long it would take to reach the rendezvous, so just after seven o'clock we strolled out of the hotel, crossed the main road and joined the queue for our tram. At the third stop we jumped down, watching the other passengers who got off, found the right bus stop and did not have long to wait. Although we recognised none of the faces on the bus, at the end of the line we dawdled so as to be the last to leave and then stood in the square chatting until everyone had departed.

From one side of the square a broad street rose steeply. The left-hand side was lined with lofty and massive old buildings set behind a high wall, which from where we stood looked continuous. As we were still about twenty minutes early, we sauntered past the bottom of the hill and all round the square. When, in the gathering dusk, we began to stroll uphill following the wall, we could see that tall wooden gates were set into it at regular intervals.

We had gone only a hundred yards or so when one of these gates swung inwards and two pairs of arms whisked us through into a dark yard and closed the gate behind us. A few hushed words from unseen faces reassured us and we were propelled up an outer metal stairway, up one indoor staircase after another, and then along a dimly-lit corridor at the end of which we paused at a door on the left. A knock, a crack of light, a murmur and the door was thrown open and closed again behind us. We were immediately engulfed in a whirl of smiling faces, cheering voices and the smells of wine, brandy and dark toasted tobacco. We were in somebody's apartment. It was so crammed with anglophile participants that we could hardly move.

There were more than twenty of us in this small living-room. Peter and I were given fierce drinks, which this time we sipped slowly, and were made to take the places of honour in the two old armchairs by the fireplace while most of the others sat on the floor, on the rim of the stout table or on the arms of chairs. A few had to stand, and changed places every so often, and I later noticed that our hosts took turns to keep watch. A spokesman apologised for the cloak-and-dagger approach and said they could find no other way of obtaining a chance to communicate freely.

There followed a two-hour period of intense conversation, almost interrogation, during which together and separately Peter and I supplied up-to-date information about Britain and – as far as we were able to comment on such matters – world affairs. It was the younger ones who were concerned about the world at large, the more senior teachers being interested in things British. One of those who had been to England in the '30s asked whether you could still buy 'Gold Flake' cigarettes, and 'Balkan Sobranie' tobacco. Another old-timer asked whether the Southern Railway was still running and, when I said it was, murmured with a sniff and a distant smile, "Ah, I can still smell the carriages". Film-stars of the '40s were discussed, wartime songs sung or hummed, various products mentioned. When I took out my Swan Vestas to light a cigarette, an older gentleman pounced on the box with a cry of recognition, and I left it with him. The conspiratorial atmosphere and the reminiscences, aided by the brandy, made for a touchingly intimate evening, at the end of which Peter and I found ourselves emotionally warmed and yet drained of energy.

We were affectionately shepherded back to an almost empty bus-stop and given careful directions. These were elaborated once again when our bus drew up. In the rear seat we turned to watch the departure of our two shepherds, who had clearly drunk much more than we had. With their arms around each other's shoulders they meandered to the foot of the hill, swivelled uncertainly, began to stagger uphill and passed out of sight.

5: TWO KINDS OF COWARDICE

Take a map of East Africa, find where Mombasa stands facing the Indian Ocean and run your finger a little northwards along the coast. You'll come to the mouth of the Tana river. Now trace the river upstream until you reach the southern foothills of Mount Kenya and you'll see the town of Embu, tucked between two tributary streams. It was just below the point where those streams meet that my life almost came to a violent end one evening in 1972.

I was teaching in Makerere University, Kampala, under a Vice-Chancellor soon to be murdered by henchmen of Idi Amin, who would then make himself Chancellor. Uganda was just beginning to tear itself apart, relations with Kenya and Tanzania were becoming strained and the East African Community was breaking up. My wife hadn't mentioned the town of Embu, but when vacation time arrived I did agree with her that it seemed a good idea to visit Kenya while it was still possible. We packed food and clothing and set out one morning in our Volkswagen 'beetle'. Once out of the campus gates I drove alongside Bat Valley, where the clusters of huge creatures hanging high in the lofty trees to our right looked like blackened fruits rather than fruit-eating bats. Once we were through Kampala town centre, we sped eastwards around Lake Victoria, over the Victoria Nile and on to the border post at Busia. No trouble there. Then on again into Kenya skirting the lake, really a great inland sea, and across a stretch of low flat country to the town of Kisumu, nestling beside a sheltered gulf of the great lake.

Here, as we had done before when I was visiting those of my trainees who were doing their teaching-practice in Kenyan schools, we stayed the night at Eddie's place. Eddie was a Goan in his fifties who in one little shophouse ran a tiny bar, a small restaurant and a hotel comprising three or four narrow rooms that could, I had been told with a nudge and a wink, be rented by the hour. He was disarmingly frank in his conversation, and was especially fond of those topics traditionally avoided by the English: sex, religion and politics.

By the time we left the following morning, we knew the names of all the preparations he had tried in attempting to rouse his flagging libido. We heard about the one that had worked so well that he had been obliged for his mistress' sake to cool his ardour by using a certain cream. We had nodded encouragingly as he related how this had maintained his erection for hours and listened sympathetically when he explained that unfortunately the cream had turned out to have an anaesthetic as well as an uplifting effect.

We also heard how, unlike his late father, he didn't often go to the Hindu temple and how, unlike his dear dead mother, he seldom went to Kisumu's Catholic church. When he especially needed something, he would prostrate himself in the temple to seek the assistance of Shiva before strolling into the church to sit down and negotiate with God. Here his opening gambit, he said, would be worded like this: 'Now look here, God, I don't know whether you exist or not. If you do, you'll know that I've just been praying for something at the temple, but to be on the safe side I'm asking you too. Belt *and* braces, old chap. So if you do exist, just listen. I am urgently in need of...' and here he would state his demands, hinting that if God failed to satisfy them His credibility would no doubt suffer. (If his demands *were* met, I wondered, how would he know whether to thank Shiva or God? But I said nothing.) In his political views Eddie was not so equivocal, and if some of his pronouncements had reached the ears of Idi Amin, Eddie's sexual antics – if not his very life – would surely have been cut short.

On the way from Kisumu to the Rift Valley and Lake Nakuru a change of plan came about, and things started going wrong. Instead of going straight along the valley to Nairobi, said my wife, we could turn off left and go up into the Aberdares and stay at the lodge in the National Park; then we could go on to Embu and visit her old flame Charlie, who was teaching in a secondary school there. I turned left, but by the time we found the lodge the day was fading and it was raining, and we now discovered that there was no room available. Before driving back down again, I noticed that the map showed a dotted short cut, a route that would lead to Embu via Thika. As the main road was far back, I stopped the car when I reached the spot where the Thika road ought to have started and found out from some villagers where it was. Driving in the direction they pointed out, I came to a fork and stopped again. Left or right? In the gathering dusk, I managed to ascertain from a nervous passer-by that both roads went to Thika but the one on the right was new.

Naturally I took that one. It was only after driving a kilometre or so that I realised *how* new the road was and that history (however recent) was repeating itself – ten years earlier, as the reader will know, I had made a similar mistake on the way from Cambodia to Bangkok.

This road was beginning to look as if the bulldozers had only just finished. It was a single undulating track through the forest; the earth was soft, there were deep troughs where some four-wheel drive vehicle had gone through and standing pools wherever the track dipped. By now it was pitch dark. The track was too narrow for me to turn my beetle around, and if I attempted to reverse, the car would probably slide off into the undergrowth. There was nothing to do but go ahead.

It was not until hours later that we arrived in pitch darkness on the edge of the silent, sleeping town of Thika. On the way we'd had to get out of the car with a flashlight on many a rise to see where the track led or to gather branches to strew across pools at the bottom of the slopes. When, dead tired, I finally saw in the headlights a small stone bridge, I pulled up on a strip of hard flat ground nearby. We lowered the front seats and slept.

In the bright early morning light, we saw women standing in the stream below the bridge doing their washing in the clear cold water, slapping wet garments on smooth stones, laughing and chatting and spreading their laundry out on boulders to dry. My clothes were filthy, but I was not in a mood to join the happy washday throng. After a snack from our dwindling supplies we set off for Embu, found the school where Charlie was teaching and parked the car outside the small wooden house he occupied on the school campus. Charlie was a tall, good-looking, well-built, athletic figure dressed in clean shirt and shorts. I soon learnt that he spent a lot of his spare time climbing Mount Kenya. Although he was pleased to see us and was a good host, I found myself resenting him more and more as we sat around talking, eating and drinking on that first night.

The next morning he lent me a squash racquet. I hadn't played for some years, so in the hot open-air court he, being years younger than I was, much taller and very much fitter, gave me the worst thrashing I'd ever suffered. I'm not usually a bad loser in sports, but I remember that defeat. After lunch when I wouldn't have minded a siesta, his idea was that we should all go to the Tana river to see the beginnings of the dam being constructed and then go to a small waterfall a short way upriver. For some forgotten reason we went off in two cars. Although the half-built dam was uninteresting to me, Charlie lingered there, so it was late in the afternoon when, having followed him in the reddish haze his vehicle raised, the dust settled and we could see that the road had come to an end at a clearing on the bank of the Tana.

The far side of the river looked flat and marshy, but this side was bordered by a boulder-strewn slope above which was a strip of low vegetation. Where the bank levelled out, there were some trees and a footpath, above which the ground rose again into open scrubland. We set out on foot along a narrow path that ran near the trees and roughly parallel to the river, my wife chatting with Charlie about old times while I followed, a little nervously, a yard or two behind. To our right were the rocks and water, to our left the grassy rise studded here and there with shrubs and small trees. The sun was getting low; I was getting anxious.

"How far away *is* this waterfall, Charlie?" I asked.

"Oh, not far now. About fifteen minutes, that's all."

He was near enough right. We came to a spot just below the waterfall, nosed around, then sat down and chatted. After a while I suggested we ought to be thinking about returning to the cars, but this was ignored. I felt like returning to the VW alone and waiting there, but I didn't want to appear timid in the presence of the intrepid Charlie; so I followed him

31

down to a little inlet where the water was still. In the mud at the water's edge, dark and damp, I could see the imprint of some very large paws. In the pale dried mud at my feet there were depressions that could surely only be elephant footprints. I pointed these out and said again that perhaps we should be getting back. This time my suggestion was accepted, though with ill grace; and I scrambled up to the winding path intent on setting the pace. That was why I was alone when I came face to face with the elephant.

The river was now on my left, and behind the grassy rise on my right the light was beginning to fade. Silhouetted against the sky were what I took to be a group of shrubs, until some of them moved, whereupon I could make out three or four elephants browsing. They were still about a quarter of a mile away but slowly moving towards the river, so I turned and shouted to the others, unseen round a bend in the track, to get a move on. That shout may well have saved my life.

Before I could take another step, there came a loud thrashing of branches from the undergrowth a short distance ahead, near the river. Then came an ear-splitting crack, a splintering of timber and a great swishing as a sizeable tree crashed onto the path about thirty yards in front of me, and out of the undergrowth stepped a huge well-tusked bull elephant.

Swivelling to face me, he flapped his great ears, raised his trunk, lowered his head and charged. For a second or two, I was incapable of anything as exhausting as thought, let alone movement. I stood transfixed. The elephant could have trampled me into an unrecognisable mess, but he stopped about a dozen yards away and snorted foul air and dust all over me. Only then did my mind snap into action. Backpedalling a few yards, I found myself next to the huge trunk of a providential baobab tree, stepped to the left so as to hide behind it and yelled again.

"Get off the path! Elephant! Get off the path!"

This leading elephant was on the path between us and the cars, but the slope to my left between the trees and the river was steep and rocky. Surely an elephant couldn't charge down there? That was the place to go. My wife appeared out of the bushes.

"Quick, down here!" I hissed.

"Where's Charlie gone?"

"*Sod* Charlie. Come on!"

We scampered down almost to the water's edge and then turned right and began to clamber over large riverside boulders, making our way back towards the cars and keeping as much distance as possible between ourselves and the path. From somewhere out in the river came the half-roar, half-belch of a hippopotamus. It took some time to reach the flat area where the cars were parked. I raced across the open ground to unlock the VW, but my wife took her time. She had seen that Charlie was lounging in his car waiting for us and looking nonchalant.

A little later I was silently accusing myself of being 'yellow' on two counts: firstly because I didn't have sufficient courage to obey my own instincts, leave the others and go back to my car; and secondly because, unlike Charlie, I had been absolutely petrified when the elephant charged. Later still, I pronounced myself not guilty on the second count. Charlie let slip that elephants always make a preliminary warning charge. I hadn't known that.

6: DANNY

Cancer? Murder? Motorway smash? Plane crash?

"Terrible, but it won't happen to me," we say to ourselves.

I suppose there must be some very primitive reason why, however great the dangers around us, we go about our daily business assuming that this is the case. Even when the net begins to close in and it happens to acquaintances or colleagues, we tend to carry on much as usual, taking refuge in that blithe assumption. I did so myself, until it happened to Danny. Quiet, good-natured, carefree Danny.

Danny was a junior member of staff in the Department of Language Methods, Makerere University, when I arrived in Kampala as the new Head of Department in 1971, a few months after the coup that ousted the President of Uganda, Milton Obote. The crowds had danced and cheered in the streets of Kampala when Obote had fled and taken refuge in neighbouring Tanzania. They had wildly welcomed his successor, a huge northerner, a Kakwa who had completed only a few years of primary schooling before joining the King's African Rifles. As a boxer, he had then won the national heavyweight boxing championship and retained the title for almost two decades; and as a soldier, he had risen in the ranks to become head of Obote's sinister security force, the General Service Unit. He was Idi Amin Dada.

When he had taken over in January 1971, there had been cheers. Within months these had given way to fears. Certain public figures, including the Supreme Court judge, had (as we expatriates put it) 'been disappeared'. Bodies would be found (if at all) days later, whole or dismembered, dumped in fields not far from the university or sometimes in a burnt-out car left smouldering in a roadside ditch just outside town. Any doctor who after an autopsy pronounced that a charred victim had been shot in the head before the 'accident' would in turn 'be disappeared'.

Up to this time Uganda had been called 'the pearl of Africa' because its climate was pleasant, its soils rich, its agricultural produce excellent, its topography varied and in places very picturesque, its wildlife abundant and its peoples reasonably well-fed and happy. Things were clearly changing for the worse, but Makerere was still widely acknowledged as the best university in sub-Saharan Africa – witness the fact that those of my students who came from Britain, Australia or elsewhere in the Commonwealth would have their qualifications recognised in their home countries. I was responsible for training teachers of languages (not just English but also French, German, Kiswahili and Luganda). English was the medium of schooling in most subjects, so when the Faculty of Education's trainees went out on teaching-practice, I joined my other colleagues in supervising student-teachers of all subjects – Agriculture, Biology, Chemistry, Geography, History and Mathematics, for example – not just foreign languages. It was a job that kept me on my professional toes.

There was the added attraction of driving all over Uganda and even into Kenya to visit the trainees in the schools. There was the pleasure of drawing back the curtains in an upcountry hotel and finding a crested crane on the lawn a few feet away; and there was the exhilaration of driving round a bend and almost into the path of a herd of giraffe galloping across the road. On that occasion my Volkswagen beetle skidded to a halt only just in time, and I gaped at the legs thundering past the windscreen, peered up at the towering heads and thanked my lucky stars that I hadn't reached the spot a few seconds earlier. A giraffe can kill a lion with one kick.

Back on the campus, the sound of automatic gunfire would sometimes drift across the valley at night to remind us academics on Makerere Hill that people were being killed. But they were people I didn't know, and the rhythms of Congolese pop-music would soon start up again in Suzanna's nightclub and come floating across half a mile of warm dark air to comfort us.

In September 1972, about a year after my arrival and some weeks after the Uganda *Argus* had started carrying articles hostile to the country's Asian population, Idi Amin announced the imminent expulsion of the Asians. Whether Hindu, Moslem or Sikh, these were mostly holders of British passports who had been born in Uganda. No exception was made for people like a bewildered old lady born there in the 1880s. Now events were affecting people that I knew well. Asian colleagues started packing in a hurry, for the African's long-standing resentment of the enterprising Asian was expressing itself in violence. My next-door neighbour, certain that Amin would not last long, completely filled one of my bedrooms with his personal library and, with his English wife and child, left with a hopeful 'au revoir'.

Amin had early on made it clear that the university was not a sacrosanct ivory tower. He had dismissed the Vice-Chancellor appointed by Obote and installed Frank Kalimuzo, a thoughtful and friendly man who one day discussed with me the problems of English-teaching in Uganda. But the net was closing in. Two days later Frank received in his campus house an urgent telephone message. A military vehicle had entered the campus and an army officer demanded to know his whereabouts. The warning was too late: he was driven away and never seen again, alive or dead. Amin then appointed himself as Chancellor and my Dean as Vice-Chancellor. I happened to be with the Dean when this appointment came through; it was then that I discovered that fear can drain as much colour from a shiny brown African skin as from a rosy English complexion. The net was drawing in closer and closer, but still I felt invulnerable.

I should explain that being a white, a 'mzungu', I was not a particular target. True, a pair of American reporters had come to a nasty end in an army barracks, but that was because they had been investigating a 'disappearance'. Far more at risk were two groups of Africans: those decent, honourable Ugandans who asked awkward questions or expressed objections to what was going on, and anyone connected with Tanzania. Tanzania had welcomed the ousted Obote, and Tanzania's army had now, in September 1972, invaded Uganda, advanced towards Kampala and was only about fifty miles away. My closest colleague Matt Mosha was a Tanzanian.

One fine morning I left my campus house as usual and walked downhill to the Faculty of Education. Because the foundation of the building was cut into a steep slope, the roadway above it curled to the left in a tight curve and swept down to the basement on the far side, where the main entrance stood; but anyone coming down on foot had only to walk straight along the raised footway that led into an upper storey of the building. As I approached the building on foot that particular morning a small camouflaged troop-carrier came speeding past me, slowed and swept downhill towards the main entrance.

"My God," I thought, "they've come to pick up Matt."

I started running. Down the outside steps, into the corridor, from room to room.

"Where's Matt? Anyone seen Matt?"

No one knew where he was. Perhaps he was still at home. I telephoned. No answer. I was re-dialling when a Ugandan colleague came into my office and told me what had just happened. The soldiers had taken away our young technician, the ever-smiling Danny. Anyone unfortunate enough to be carted off by the military was as good as dead, for it was now well-known that the army made no distinction between interrogation and torture, execution and sadistic savagery. None of us could imagine Danny committing any offence so serious as to merit such a ghastly end.

Taken to a military complex like Makindye Military Police HQ, the prisoner was invariably put through a mockery of the legal process, found guilty of some crime such as attempting to prevent an officer from stealing his car or wife and, if he was lucky, merely executed. One normal method of executing 'traitors' was as follows. A file of handcuffed prisoners would be marched out at gunpoint in the darkness and halted at a certain spot. The first in line was the luckiest: he was made to lie flat on the hard ground while the second was given a sledgehammer and forced to smash the waiting head, hand the sledgehammer on to number three and lie down himself in the sticky mess. So it would go on down the line, the smirking NCO being obliged to despatch only the last man.

In the next few days I kept hoping that Danny would turn up one morning, grin sheepishly and tell us how he had been mistakenly arrested; but as the days and weeks went by, I accepted the conclusion already reached by my colleagues. We wouldn't be seeing Danny again.

Then, almost two months after his arrest, Danny returned from the dead with a gaunt face and infrequent wan smile. He seemed in reasonable health and we all made a fuss of him, which he didn't like, and said how wonderful it was to have him back. Danny quietly and solemnly agreed that his deliverance was a miracle. There were certain things he wouldn't talk about, but we eventually pieced the story together.

Some months previously a country friend of his had turned up in town and asked Danny to put him up for a day or two in his modest campus quarters. Danny had consented and, leaving his friend at home, had gone off to work the following morning wearing a pair of rather gaudy trainers he had just bought in the market. Later that same morning the military police had turned up and found the place empty but discovered a holdall containing a military uniform. They made a few enquiries and went to the Department to get Danny. Danny said he knew nothing about the uniform. Whether he ever named his friend we never found out, but he was taken off for further questioning in the Makindye HQ. The officer on duty that day must have had a quite intimate knowledge of Makerere because he asked detailed and pertinent questions, and it was dark by the time he ordered the duty sergeant to take Danny to one of the cells. With his carbine pointing at Danny and his torch pointing the way along a path, the sergeant smartly marched Danny away. About what happened in the days that followed Danny was uncommunicative; but when he told us what occurred some weeks later, he showed the whites of his eyes as the lids widened with remembered terror.

Late one night he and a number of fellow prisoners were roughly roused, pushed outside and assembled in a shivering line under the twinkling stars. On a given order they turned right and were marched off into darkness, guided by the swinging beam of a flashlight. They halted. Outside the pounding of blood in Danny's ears there was a long silence, then a murmur of voices and the sound of heavy steps approaching. Then a shout close to his ear made him jump.

"*You!*"

His heart pounding fit to burst, Danny was dragged out of the line. His dry throat strangled a cry of protest. His legs had given way and the toes of his nice new trainers were scraping the ground as the strong hands gripping his upper arms carried him along. Then it began to dawn on him that he was being manhandled back to his cell. His initial relief quickly gave way to the fear that he was being saved for some more exquisite form of execution, and he passed a night of dread, by turns imagining and praying; but when morning came, he was astounded to find that he was being set free.

It was then that he discovered how this release had come about. There had been an almost incredible sequence of coincidences. It had so happened that the officer on duty when Danny had first been brought in was an intelligent and conscientious man who did follow up the case, which many officers would not have bothered to do. It also happened that the sergeant who had marched him to his cell that night was, unlike many NCOs, efficient and obedient. His officer had told him that he was convinced Danny had been arrested by mistake and that he should therefore come to no harm. However, the wheels of military administration ground slowly; the duty rosters changed from day to day; weeks passed, and Danny learned which guards to fear most and which officers were least conscientious and reliable. It was one of these officers who eventually included Danny's name in a list of prisoners condemned to death; but then came more coincidences.

On the night appointed for the execution of those on that particular list it was the turn of both the conscientious officer and the efficient sergeant to be on duty together again. The officers, especially perhaps the more humane ones, tended to leave such unpleasant duties to the sergeants, who in turn delegated as much as possible to corporals. Neither the officer nor his sergeant was present when the prisoners were hauled out of their cells, but the sergeant did check the number being marched off. In the light of a corporal's torch he caught sight of a distinctive pair of trainers and, remembering where he had seen them before, told the corporal to halt the file of prisoners. He then ran back to check with the duty officer, who ordered him to put Danny back in his cell.

Danny's release had come through a few days later. To me, the story was one of fortunate coincidences; but to him, the believer who had prayed in his cell, it was nothing short of a miracle for which God had to be praised. Might it be that a certain constellation of coincidences is what a miracle consists of?

7: Nowhere to Turn

When Field Marshal Idi Amin Dada had insulted Her Majesty Queen Elizabeth and exasperated her Government once too often, diplomatic relations between Britain and Uganda were severed. Among other things this meant that, although I had signed a three-year contract to teach in Makerere until the end of the academic year in 1974, my salary as from a given date in '73 would no longer contain the large supplement provided by my government through the Inter-University Council. I wouldn't be able to fulfil my family commitments on the local salary, which was far too low, so I had to make preparations to leave Uganda a year early. The trouble was, I couldn't return to my permanent job in Manchester because I had released it to someone else for all three years. I'd have to go back to England and look for a one-year job to fill the gap.

When the time came for me and my wife to leave Kampala, most of the country's industries and public facilities had broken down. I had to buy some wood and construct my own crate before packing it myself and arranging for it to go as air freight from Entebbe to Manchester airport. In order to leave legally, it was necessary to complete seventeen different forms, all of them in triplicate or quadruplicate. Some were for permission to sell the 18-month-old Beetle (for more than I'd paid for it, because imports had stopped), some for permission to leave the country, some for permission to close my bank account and so on. Then, when we at last took my flimsy-looking openwork crate to the airport, there was a partial solar eclipse. Entebbe is only about fifty miles from the equator, and the afternoon light is usually intense; but the temperature dipped and the sun dimmed, draining much of the colour from Lake Victoria and the surrounding vegetation and making the little airport look as flat as a stage backdrop. This didn't seem a good omen; and sure enough, back in England it proved impossible to find a teaching job in ELT for just one year. First my short leave petered out, then my savings. Not knowing which way to turn next, I went on the dole.

Job-hunting paid off. A few weeks later I found an advertisement for the post of 'Unesco Expert in English' in Aden, applied, was interviewed by a Unesco-Overseas Development Agency panel and given the job. I've always disliked the word 'expert' when used in the context of education, but I certainly didn't quibble about this when I went to the Paris HQ of Unesco and was briefed in a grand *château*. My salary was far too high, and I got the impression that the headquarters staff was spending more money on itself than in the world's poorest countries.

Of these, the People's Democratic Republic of South Yemen was one of the most impoverished. In Aden as in Kampala things were literally falling apart – the bathroom in the Crescent Hotel, the college buildings where I was teaching at Khormaksar, the air-conditioning units everywhere, the balcony of our flat. There were small sand-dunes in the college language laboratory, and rats ran about in the little adjoining room that was my study. Outside, in Khormaksar, Ma'alla and Crater, it seemed to me that nothing had been replaced, repaired or repainted in the six years since the British had pulled out. A 'republic', I had learned in a Latin lesson at school, was *res publica*, the business of the people; and *demos* was the Greek word for 'the people'. A Democratic Republic was therefore The People's Business of the People, so the *People's Democratic Republic of South Yemen*... well, methought the title did protest too much. In place of the British it was now the Russians who were controlling and exploiting the people, and the East Germans were helping to set up a police state.

Here were the shortages and queues that I had seen in Hungary, for the Soviet system of centralisation and nationalisation was operating. Soap would be unavailable for a whole month, for example, during which time the only vegetables on sale would be cabbages; then the shops would be full of soap and there would be no meat in the market. Shortly after I arrived in 1973, the plentiful lobsters disappeared completely from the market, never to return. The locals privately made up simple jokes against the régime. One was about a fisherman who during a day's toil caught nothing and came into port wailing, "No fish, no fish! The sea has been nationalised!"

I'll come back to the poor fish later.

When I first arrived in that rainless, hot, humid, dusty place, the creatures I felt sorriest for – apart from the people, of course – were the crows. Europeans aren't usually sympathetic towards the carrion crow, which scavenges and feeds on dead and rotting flesh. But this hooded subspecies, its body cigarette-ash grey and the rest black – what could it find to eat, and where in this barren and almost treeless area could it nest? And what in any case could it use as nesting-material? I soon discovered some answers.

Night after night a rat had been raiding the kitchen of my seedy and sandy first-floor flat, ignoring the trap I'd set and gnawing into bags, packets and even canned foods. When I eventually found places for our food that the rat couldn't reach, it carried off a bar of soap, so further supplies of this too had to be made inaccessible. Someone advised me to put chocolate in the trap instead of cheese, and this worked first time. The rat was huge. I picked the lifeless body up by its tail, opened the kitchen window, swung the thing round a few times and let go. As it sailed over the back wall towards a stretch of waste ground, two hooded crows swooped down from the roof and were on to it the moment it thudded into the dust. When I looked out a few minutes later, there was nothing left.

The same pair of crows decided to nest in a dead tree just below my crumbling balcony, one of the few available places; but once they had stuffed a few bits of paper and plastic wrapping into the chosen fork, there was nothing else to build with. The dead twigs under the tree had been gathered for firewood, and for miles around there was nothing green except, here and there, flaking paint. Then they discovered the chain-link fencing. The winds from the nearby Indian Ocean picked up salty sand and deposited it around the building, and the sea breeze blew the finer stuff through the rusted mosquito netting and into the flat; that was why the tree below was dead and nothing grew around the building any more. Even the plastic-coated wire of the fence was not immune from these corrosive effects, and the crows somehow found out that occasional bits of wire could be bent back and forth, broken off and wriggled out of the mesh. There was a great deal of cawing and fluttering, and in no time a bowl-shaped nest of wire appeared in the fork of the dead tree. From my unsafe balcony I was soon looking down at four bluish, brown-blotched eggs in it; the Russian living downstairs then took a pole and destroyed the whole thing. Because I felt sorry for the oppressed Adeni people, who were managing to survive amidst severe shortages, this act seemed to me in some way symbolic. It was not long, though, before I was feeling sorry for the fish rather than the crows.

A tiny, slender silver fish lifted its head and once more beat its tail a few times on the hot stone. The black claws spread across it did not move, but a black-cowled head bent down and turned so that one glassy dispassionate eye could examine the captive, while the other faced a midday sky that was white with heat and humidity except for a little faint bluishness directly overhead. Raising its head again, the hooded crow looked left and right along the shimmering crescent of beach. There others of its kind awaited the next offering.

Sure enough, a turbulence in the shallows produced a sudden glittering cascade, and dozens of little fish, most of them little longer than a crow's beak, fell flapping onto the burning sand or slithered over the hot smooth stones where the crows were lining up, waiting close to the water's edge but never letting the gently slopping, soupy sea touch them. There was a flurry of black wings, a waddling of black legs and a stamping of black claws, then stillness until another silver shower further along stirred the more distant birds into similar action. I hadn't realised there were so many crows in Aden.

Though the shallows were only a few inches deep, the water was so turbid that I could seldom see what was going on under the surface, except when a sudden dull glint told me that in their panic another shoal of small fry had suddenly wheeled away from hidden danger. Somewhere in the tepid soup that slipped over the sand and lapped against the hot stones colonised by the crows, razor-toothed predators were slicing a hungry way through those tiny swerving slivers of silver. Some of the fugitives, soaring above the water, slipped back into it and made good their escape; others, unless gathered up by a succeeding wavelet, were left out of their element to die stranded on the burning shore. Some of those that had landed near my feet a few minutes ago already lay lifeless, dull and shrivelled on the sizzling stones, ready-cooked but unclaimed.

I wondered why the intelligent hooded crows didn't just gather up these fresh sun-baked fish rather than stand around waiting to catch fresh ones of their own. It wasn't as if the newly-stranded youngsters were immediately gobbled up as fresh delicacies; once a crow had stepped on a fish, much as a man might stamp on a dropped coin, it would simply stand on it and wait for it to die. Nor did any crow ever attempt to pick up a living fish in its beak. Too slimy, perhaps? Maybe, but that was not true of those dead fugitives already drying out around the shoreline.

I was sitting in the shade, dressed only in swimming-trunks but sweating profusely. Having left my clothes in the suffocatingly hot cement-lined changing-room, I'd ordered a beer as I'd passed the little kiosk that served as an open-air bar. I had then hopped swiftly over pale hot sand that seared my soles and followed the intermittent strip of shade provided by a short line of beachside shelters. The one at the far end was open to what little breeze existed, but by the time I had reached it I was already drenched with sweat. I had run my cupped hands upwards over my stomach and chest to scoop away the sweat, flicked a couple of handfuls on to the sand, draped my towel over a bright blue plastic chair and sat down to face the water and watch these crows.

I was still watching when a figure in baggy white trousers and loose shirt appeared with the large bottle of beer I had ordered. Unfamiliar label. St Pauli Girl. East German. I settled the bill and took a long cool draught. Hm, not bad. Sitting back, I looked across part of the little bay towards the few small buildings that constituted the Gol Mohur Club. It was a fenced-off relic of British days that still served as a swimming club but was now somewhat ramshackle. It was the only place in the country, apart from the private pools on the premises of Cable and Wireless and Shell, where women could appear outdoors in swimming costume. The club was named after the Gol Mohur tree, whose blossoms are flame-red.

Facing me on the far side of the sandy bay was the gate through which I had driven. My little olive-green Datsun Cherry was parked nearby, along with a couple of other cars, under the thin shade of some pale trees that seemed to be dead. To one side stood the dilapidated brick office, kiosk and changing-rooms. Following the arc of the beach came the line of palm-thatched shelters leading up to the last, the one I was sitting under.

Beyond this point, to my other side, the beach gave way to a low rocky outcrop from which a sea wall had been built across the bay. It consisted of boulders topped with a flat concrete surface and ran straight across, except for a gap of a few feet in the middle left to let the tide in and out and prevent the swimming area from stagnating. At high tide the wall stood in water about ten feet deep. Not until the tide began to go out could you see the stout steel mesh of a shark-net that spanned the gap. A few yards from the far end of the wall stood the Club gate and parked cars. The swimming area, then, was bounded by a semicircle of sand and a straight sea-wall which together formed a huge capital D. My seat at the bottom of the D provided me with a clear view of the whole.

The tide had come in, bringing with it a fleet of dark, torpedo-shaped fish as long as my forearm. I had glimpsed one or two of these in the shallows; they moved like greased lightning. From the swirling of the water and unending silver showers of fish, I could tell that there were dozens of these killers gorging themselves down there. Around the shore, the hooded crows were gorging too, waiting for each victim to die, pulling it apart and then, beaks pointing at the sky, jerkily swallowing the pieces.

As I watched the fish under submarine attack and land offensive, a squadron of brilliant white terns, elegant sea swallows with long slender wings and long forked tails, flew overhead and gathered over the middle of the D-shaped bay. Fluttering and swirling down to a height of twenty feet or so, they hovered beak-down, half-folded their wings and dived like snow-white Stukas. Each one plunged vertically as straight as an arrow into the water and immediately rose again, almost always with a little fish twinkling in its beak. The first jerk of the neck would ensure that the fish lay in the beak with its head towards the gullet, the second would seal its fate. Only twice did I see a tern drop its prey. On both occasions the bird corkscrewed down and caught the fish in mid-air.

The slaughter went on and on long after I'd finished my bottle of St Pauli Girl and had consequently begun to sweat even more profusely. Maybe the beer also made me fanciful, but this scene too seemed to me symbolic. The people of Aden and the surrounding territory had jumped from the British frying-pan into the Soviet fire. They had wriggled and shied away and wished themselves elsewhere. Some of them – such as the vendor who had sidled up to me in the market, made an obscene gesture and whispered "Roosski fookoff" – even wished that the British were still running things. But like the little fish, they now seemed to have nowhere to turn.

8: Aboard a Burning Plane

I suppose we can all tell of an episode in our lives when things seemed to gang up against us: the weather, timetables, solid objects, people around – anything and everything. It's a phenomenon enshrined in the English language, in the adage 'Troubles come in threes', in the proverb 'It never rains but it pours' and in the popular concept labelled variously 'Murphy's Law', 'Sod's Law' or 'The Universal Law of Buggerability'. My own tale of woe concerns a trip to the island of Borneo in 1978. It is largely a catalogue of Persistent Pains and Perverse Planes.

At the request of The British Council, I was going there to advise on what English-teaching posts, if any, should be established in Sabah and Sarawak, the two Malaysian states on that vast and fascinating island. For administrative purposes, it was necessary to go via Kuala Lumpur, situated on what has to be called 'the mainland', even though the area of the two Bornean states is fifty percent greater than that of peninsular Malaysia. It was an aircraft that attacked first.

Perverse Plane Number One struck even before I had cleared customs at Kuala Lumpur airport. All the other passengers had long since gathered their luggage and departed, but my one large suitcase had not appeared. I informed one of the ground staff, was taken to an office, filled in a form and waited. The suitcase was one of those smart fibreglass-and-aluminium models with an average depth of about eight inches. When a smiling official eventually appeared and put it on the office counter, most of it was still eight inches deep. The rest, about a quarter of it, was approximately an inch thick. It had, I was informed, fallen off a vehicle on the runway and been run over by a taxi-ing plane. The official was still grinning.

"But that's ruined!" I exclaimed rather superfluously. "I can't even get it open! I'll have to buy another one here. *And* replace any damaged goods inside."

I was smilingly handed a form on which to list, when I was able to open the case, the nature and value of anything damaged; to this I should append receipts for anything replaced. I went out of the airport to find an agitated but relieved Council driver still waiting for me. He too grinned at my suitcase, heaved it into the boot and drove me into town to meet Persistent Pain Number One, a Council officer whom I shall call Brian. He was a pain in, shall we say, the neck. After initial greetings in his office, I realised that he had only three topics of conversation. Not quite the traditional list of wine, women and song, because he wasn't musical; with him it was sex, alcohol and money, usually in that order. And he talked almost non-stop.

Once in the privacy of my hotel room, I managed to wrench my suitcase open and discovered that miraculously none of my personal goods had suffered noticeable damage. That afternoon I managed to buy from a grinning shopkeeper a far superior case for half the amount he at first asked, which in turn was about half of what I had paid for my now half-mangled model. I also persuaded him to give me a receipt for the amount he had originally demanded. Back at the hotel I filled in the form, attached the receipt and smiled at the considerable amount that would be refunded to me. That, I thought, was nothing more than poetic justice. So much for Perverse Plane Number One.

I still had to deal with Brian, who was about to pick me up and take me to a semi-formal dinner. His call came through much earlier than expected: he was waiting for me downstairs in the hotel bar. I dutifully dressed and descended.

"Ah, Gerry! What'll you have?"

"Um, a Tiger. Thanks."

"Nothing stronger? Chota peg?"

"No, a beer will do fine, thanks."

When he had ordered my beer and his double whisky, he looked at his watch and got down to business.

"Well, it's only just after six and we're not expected till eight at the earliest. I thought we might have a couple of these and go down to this club I belong to. Best in KL, I reckon. Women are fantastic, whisky's reasonable, membership's very cheap as these things go, and I'm allowed one guest."

"Well, I – "

"I'm *telling* you. Those Malay women down there, they'll do anything you want." He leaned forward over the low table, an unprepossessing figure with a corpulent body, a balding head and bulging eyes. "*Anything!*"

"Well, Brian, it's been a tiring day and I'm not – "

"You won't regret it, you know."

"Yes, but – "

"OK, OK. Waiter! Two more, please."

It was good to get on the plane the next morning with the thought that I'd be having a week in Sabah without his company. An hour down to Singapore, then three hours eastwards across the South China Sea to Kota Kinabalu, which everyone at the dinner had referred to as 'KK'; there I was picked up and taken to a nice old-fashioned hotel in which

Somerset Maugham would have been very much at home. For four days everything went smoothly as I was taken by LandRover to see schools and colleges outside KK and flew eastwards again to Sandakan, on a coast that faced the Philippines and was still subject to pirate raids, usually at night.

Then, back at KK on the Saturday, some friendly expatriates invited me to join them on their launch. They were going to visit a small uninhabited island a few miles away. The trip took only about half an hour, and once the launch had been tied to an overhanging palm tree, people were free to do their own thing,. I walked along the dazzling white beach, over some rocks and a little way into the island, noting various birds, lizards and butterflies. On my way back I waded in the shallows looking at the fish and creatures in the rock-pools. When the trip was over and I was back in my hotel room having a shower, my left ankle was aching a little and I noticed a puncture on it. I packed most of my things and was ready to catch Flight MH258 to Kuching the following day. There Persistent Pain Number One would be waiting.

I awoke the next morning to find that Persistent Pain Number Two had started. My ankle was swollen a little, but the slight ache was not too worrying. After giving me lunch at the Irena Yacht Club, my expat friend took me to the airfield; there we experienced some unexplained delay. We sat around talking and sipping drinks until suddenly a loudspeaker voice said, "Last call for Mister Abort". I thought I must have missed earlier calls and was now holding up the departure, so I scattered thanks and handshakes about me and scurried off to the barrier, where a slender young air hostess, very elegant in her sarong kebaya uniform, greeted me.

"You Mister Abort?"

"Yes."

"Ticket please?"

"Here you are."

"Come this way, please."

Handing the ticket to an airline colleague, she escorted me out on to the tarmac, where the usual FW27, a Fokker Friendship, was already warming up some distance away. The young air hostess was also warming up. She chatted away and said that she would like to show me round

Kuching but unfortunately had to go on to KL. Perhaps I could get in touch with her there? And she gave me a telephone number. Why this interest in an English teacher? What was behind it? I soon found out.

"You charter this plane, is it?"

"Me? *Charter* it? Good Lord, no!"

She lost her smile and looked puzzled. And disappointed.

"Why do you ask?"

"You the only passenger, so I think you charter it."

"Ha! I wish I *could* afford to charter one. I'm just a teacher."

She walked on ahead, noticeably cooler and more distant.

When I climbed onto the empty plane, a different hostess settled me in right at the back and, once airborne, asked if I would like champagne. *Champagne*? This flight was beginning to take on an unreal quality. I had had enough to drink back in KK and was feeling drowsy, so I asked for Chinese tea. Again I saw that puzzled disappointment. When she brought the tea, I asked how it was that I was the only passenger, but she managed to avoid answering. I sipped, lay back and dozed.

I awoke with an alarming smell in my nose. It was that sharp distinctive scent of burning rubber and plastic you get if there's a short circuit in the room or the electrics in your car catch fire. I must have dozed for a considerable time, for when I opened my eyes the plane was already so full of grey smoke that I couldn't see a thing. As I was wondering what I should do, the smoke by my right shoulder billowed suddenly and I felt, rather than saw, a figure rushing forward along the aisle. Leaning over, I looked out of the porthole to my left. Propellers turning normally. Port engine not on fire. Perverse Plane Number Two on an even keel and presumably on course. Sea very blue and calm far below. No land in sight.

By now my nose was running, my eyes were beginning to water and I wanted to cough; but I kept my mouth shut and held a handkerchief to my face. I heard the thump of hurried footsteps too late to be able to stop the male figure I could just make out as he hurried aft; only now did the prospect of plunging into the South China Sea occupy my thoughts. I really frightened myself. I could see mangled bodies down there, sharks feasting, bits of wreckage in the sea. The end of a beautiful Fokker Friendship. With heart beating hard, lungs panting and ankle nagging, I bemoaned the injustice of it. I'm only forty-three. Why me?

After about ten minutes, by which time I had reviewed my inadequate life and subsided into abject self-pity, the smoke began to clear. I could see the opposite porthole, then some of the seats in front, then as far as the pilot's cabin. A figure appeared in the seat to my right. It was Little Miss Golddigger.

"You okay sir?"

I wiped my eyes and nose.

"Yes. Yes thanks. It was just the smoke. What happened?"

"Happen? Oh, er, we got bit of trouble with air-con, that's all."

She was a terrible liar. I asked for more tea and was sipping this when the co-pilot came and apologised. The fault, which he carefully did not specify, had been traced and there was no further danger. I asked if the aircraft would have to be grounded at Kuching.

"Well, no. It's a pretty old aircraft, you see. We were told there were no passengers for Kuching, so we *were* going to take it straight from KK to KL for repairs and refitting. But then you turned up and there were no other aircraft available... so..."

He shrugged and departed.

Once again profit had taken precedence over safety.

I breathed a sigh of relief when Flight MH258 landed at Kuching. So much for Perverse Plane Number Two. But now Persistent Pain Number One was waiting for me at the hotel, Persistent Pain Number Two in my swelling ankle was getting worse, and I had to catch a plane to the upcountry town of Sibu in the morning.

My diary for Monday, 20 March 1978, began: 'Foot poisoned. Hurts like hell if I even touch it.' It was puffy and yellow; the veins above the ankle were a vivid red. I went to a Chinese doctor, who gave me eight capsules, two per day for the time I'd be spending upcountry.

Brian and I flew to Sibu, did an afternoon's work at a teacher training college and checked in at our hotel. That evening in the fourth floor restaurant he talked while I observed the rats running around and up the curtain behind him entirely unmolested. I had long since become used to them in Bangkok and Aden, but when at length I pointed them out, he was aghast. In the breakfast bar the following morning they were scampering from one end of the room to the other, using the bench seats as hurdles as they searched for scraps. Brian, in the bright light of day and without a brandy in his belly, was so horrified that he couldn't eat his breakfast and hardly stopped talking about it for the rest of the day. It made a change from the usual topics.

We spent most of that day at the teacher-training college and then took a riverboat to Sarikei, which was what Americans would call a one-horse town but did have a teacher's college. It was evening by the time we disembarked; my foot was killing me, and I was exhausted. We went out into town and found somewhere to eat; then I went to bed early, leaving him sitting moodily over a half-bottle of Chinese hooch labelled, perhaps appropriately, Red Cock Brandy. Before turning in, I took my tablets and looked at my leg. My foot had ballooned and the angry red lines had climbed well past my knee, too close to my genitals for comfort. Around the puncture in my foot there was a large blister-like protuberance which, when I prodded it, gave no pain. I went to the bathroom, took out a razor-blade, slit the skin, mopped up the result with toilet paper and stuck a plaster over the cut. In the morning the red lines had receded to my knee and I was able to get my left shoe on without too much pain.

That morning Brian informed me that he was unwell and would have to opt out of the day's programme. I suspected that, one way or another, he was suffering from Red Cock. I clucked sympathetically, secretly welcoming the news. That day, without the presence of Persistent Pain Number One, I was able to limp round three primary schools, a secondary school and a teacher-training college, and to have useful discussions with the staff of each one.

When I returned, the sun was low and unfortunately Brian seemed to be his normal self again. My leg felt easier, and we walked right round the town. It took fifteen minutes; I found nothing of note except a pile of golden jungle durians by the riverbank and nearby an amusing sign which read:

Express Engine Repairs
HANG ONN

After another day's work at the teacher-training college, we took the express boat back from Sarikei to Sibu on Good Friday and there boarded the plane to Kuching. By now Brian was somewhat subdued, the angry lines on my leg had subsided and my foot was almost back down to its previous size. So although my nose was giving me a bit of trouble, I felt that I had at last come through a difficult time with my standard still flying. I was counting my chickens too soon, of course, tempting Providence, forgetting that it never rains but pours, that troubles always come in threes and that the universe was subject to the implacable and immutable laws I mentioned at the outset.

On that little one-hour flight from Sibu to Kuching, Perverse Plane Number Three and Persistent Pain Number Three ganged up on me in a final assault. Brian and I were mercifully separated, and my neighbour for the flight was a Chinese gentleman, dressed in an immaculate grey suit and reading the *Far Eastern Economic Review*. As the Fokker Friendship took off, my sinuses responded by carving channels across my forehead with a kitchen knife and thumping a base drum in my brain. I was lying back with my eyes closed when the air hostess appeared. I asked for coffee, and the Chinese gentleman wanted nothing. The coffee came. My head was splitting. I raised the cup towards my lips.

At that precise moment the plane came across a pocket of nothingness and simply dropped like a stone for what must have been several hundred feet. My brain banged against my skull, the contents of my stomach surged upwards and my coffee left the cup. The black liquid hit the ceiling and, with devastating aim, fell like a doomsday rain all over my immaculate Chinese neighbour.

There is nothing one can adequately say in such circumstances, unless one speaks fluent Foochow or Mandarin or whatever; even then it would be difficult if at the time one's sinuses were slicing up one's face and one's brain had suffered a battering. I have no idea what I tried to do or say. What I do remember is waking up the following morning in my Kuching hotel and realising that my head was clear, my foot was almost back to normal and Brian, having been told that he was urgently needed in KL, had left. I smiled at the thought that I had survived all three Perverse Planes and all three Persistent Pains. Then I stopped tempting Providence. What wiped the smile off my face was the thought that perhaps troubles don't always come only in threes.

9. Zibethinus!

When the season arrived, they were suddenly all over the place. I'd been working in Sarawak for a year, and by now I knew what to do. If I went down to the old part of town early in the morning, when the river was steaming like cooling soup and a few miles upstream the forested slopes of Matang were still wrapped in coils of rising mist, I could smell them long before I found them. They had come in boatloads from some point upriver, and now they were piled like heavy ammunition on the riverside pavement near one pyramid of pale green melons and another of dark green coconuts, as if in preparation for some crazy bombardment of the Istana – the old bungalow residence of the Rajahs that still topped the low rise on the opposite bank. Once I'd smelt them, I usually wanted to buy one there and then; but sometimes I would walk on a little way to the open-air market by the bus station where the pavement was lined with cheerful Bidayuh women, each squatting behind a few choice specimens that she had just brought down, along with small bunches of herbs and vegetables, from her longhouse. These fruits were fresher and cheaper than those in the great heaps by the river; and if by now I really couldn't wait to get my hands on one, I'd squat and greet, grin and haggle and buy.

Alternatively, I could walk past these ladies and get on one of the rattly old buses waiting nearby, the one going to Serian, and get off at Kilometre 11 where I'd be sure to find roadside vendors, each with a tall basketful of the fruit. Here I could buy a few fruit much more cheaply than in town, but usually the point of coming out here was to walk up a forest path leading to one of the longhouses and, on the way, see the things growing on the trees. By now the humid air would be getting hot, and after half a mile of gentle uphill walking my shirt would be clamped to my back and my eardrums so adjusted to the continuous high shriek of the male cicada's love-song that they would tweak painfully when the racket stopped. Then I might hear ahead the chirruping of Bidayuh conversation and some pleasant laughter, and round a bend in the path above in single file would come half a dozen pretty Land Dayak women winding their way down through the trees. Across her forehead each would have a strap to take the main weight of the basket on her back, one of those tall handwoven baskets I had seen by the roadside. The young women would be in simple working clothes, just a blouse or T-shirt, a sarong and flip-flops. The baskets would be fully laden, and behind the tied-back jet-black hair I would see, showing just above their shoulders, the sharp spines of freshly-gathered fruit. As the women came near, the chattering would stop and one of them would greet me smilingly in Bidayuh or Malay in the usual way:

"Where are you going?"

"To eat the air." (That is, nowhere in particular.)

"Where do you come from?"

"From Kuching. How far is your kampong?"

"Only one cigarette. You will be welcome."

Without halting, the young woman would continue this conversation over her shoulder as everyone passed, leaving me to savour the lingering odour of their merchandise. 'One cigarette' meant about ten more minutes' climbing, and I would continue my walk.

Once, when I had stopped for a breather, I heard a rustle and a flicker of noise passing overhead and looked up. For a moment I wondered if I had contracted some fever and was hallucinating, for gliding a few feet overhead was a sizeable lizard. I watched as it slowly lost height and landed hard against the trunk of a tree some twenty yards downhill.

Walking onwards and upwards into towering trees, at a certain bend I would hear a faint splashing and see in the deep shade a glittering trickle of falling water a few yards ahead. I would find against the hillside the last of a series of carefully-arranged bamboo runnels that brought a little stream of cool spring water gently down to the level of my mouth. Underfoot, a tiny rivulet would run across the path, drop into the undergrowth and reappear as a small stream near the Serian road. It was in this rivulet that one morning I found a family of tiny vipers and had to hurry on without a drink in case one of the parents was nearby. The water itself was safe, though, and I was usually able to slake my thirst, look up into the lofty trees and see beautiful specimens of my favourite fruit far above, dozens of them, ready to fall. But they weren't mine, and it was necessary to move on.

Having reached the small longhouse and greeted those present, I would be made welcome with something to drink and perhaps a little stilted conversation before it was time to leave a little gift and go back. Passing under the great trees again on the way down, I would glance up nervously. I always felt that there was something menacing about those fruits. Cherries dangle charmingly and apples hang temptingly, but these were durians and each one impended like a raised bronze weapon – one of those heavy spiked metal balls that medieval combatants flailed and clashed onto their foes' helmets in an attempt to smash their skulls. At any time and without any effort, one of those fiercely-spined three-pounders lurking thirty feet above could achieve the same effect by silently parting company with its branch and hurtling on to the dome of my head. I remember reading in the *Borneo Bulletin* about a poor fellow who slept at the foot of his tree one night in order to protect it from fruit-thieves. In the morning his friends found him lying stone dead beneath a hole in the thatch of his makeshift shelter with a durian nestled in the ruins of his rib cage. I always felt too that there was something primeval about this monster fruit. Wasn't there some dinosaur whose tail ended in a similar spiky ball, a weapon also employed to murderous effect?

When I reached the foot of the hill, I would stop and sit by the little stream I had passed farther uphill. Here, lower down, it was the colour of lager and a yard wide, rippling over a stony bed. Dripping with sweat, I'd sit in the shade of a tree to cool off and take off my open sandals. At this point I once felt a slight tickle on the inside of my right foot just below the ankle. I found a small brown butterfly clinging there. It was rather like the Skippers I'd seen as a boy on the Surrey heathlands, heavy-bodied and with wings not closed vertically or spread horizontally but folded backwards above the abdomen. Very slowly I lifted my foot and rested it on my left knee so as to examine the creature closely.

It was so absorbed in what it was doing that it didn't move even when my face came to within a few inches of it. What I had felt was its short proboscis stirring a little puddle on my skin. Having sucked up a little pool of my mineral-rich sweat, the butterfly bent its proboscis underneath its body, between its legs and right back to its rear end, where a small drop of clear liquid emerged. The proboscis delicately picked up this tiny droplet, carried it forward underneath the body and deposited it on my skin. It now began stirring again to make a mineral soup. Fascinated, I allowed the creature to have several such meals before shooing it away, shoeing myself again and going back to the road, where the durian-sellers sat in the wayside shade.

If you have never come face to face with a durian, it is time to confess that I have been withholding something from you. Whereas your first whiff will engulf you like the heavy miasma of fresh sewage, to those who love it the same aroma will make the mouth water. Since I consider it the king of fruit, the mere thought of it now is making me salivate; but I can see that it will be difficult to persuade you to taste some, not only because its lavatorial smell will disgust you but also because its wonderful taste is so difficult to convey. I must contradict here a British friend who once said that tasting durian was like eating custard near a pile of shit; but instead of trying to describe it myself, I shall quote a great American scientist, a contemporary and equal of Charles Darwin and an undoubted duriophile. In his famous book *The Malay Archipelago*, Alfred Russel Wallace provided the finest description of the durian's flavour and texture that I know of:

> A rich butter-like custard highly flavoured with almonds gives the best general idea of it, but intermingled with it come wafts of flavour that call to mind cream-cheese, onion-sauce, brown sherry, and other incongruities. Then there is a rich glutinous smoothness in the pulp which nothing else possesses, but which adds to its delicacy. It is neither acid, nor sweet, nor juicy, yet one feels the want of none of these qualities, for it is perfect as it is. It produces no nausea or other bad effect, and the more you eat of it the less you feel inclined to stop. In fact to eat Durians is a new sensation, worth a voyage to the East to experience.

That is excellent, except that I would add that there is a sort of sulphurous warmth in the aftertaste. However, the senses of taste and smell are so intertwined that perhaps the sulphurousness is rather in its unmistakable smell, which is so pervasive and redolent of putrescence that the fruit is banned from hotels and aircraft luggage. On one of my upcountry school visits in Sarawak, a headmaster presented me with two luscious specimens to take back home to Kuching, and I took them with me when I boarded the little eight-seater monoplane for the return flight. The pilot climbed in, started up the engines and closed his window. Then he stiffened and said over his shoulder, "Someone has brought a durian on board. The passenger will please hand it to one of the ground staff." When I reluctantly slid open my window and handed my two prize specimens to a young man waiting to pull one of the chocks away, he sniffed them appreciatively, shrugged sympathetically and then, grinning from ear to ear, saluted smartly.

Wallace, clearly a connoisseur, was dead right about not being inclined to stop once you've started eating durian. With some people it's peanuts or chocolate or potato crisps, but the only thing I've ever eaten compulsively is this regal fruit. Whenever my nose led me to a spot where they were being sold, there was nothing for it but to get down on my haunches, put on a knowing air and set about selecting one or two good ones. This is easier said than done: handling something that resembles a sharply-spined cannonball with no more caution than if it were a coconut demands a degree of control over the facial muscles and vocal cords that is normally only required of royalty. Of course, you *could* just pick them up gingerly by their smooth stalks; but I never allowed myself to do this, for three good reasons: (i) none of my onlookers (by now there would be several) would have been impressed if I had begun by holding up one of those magnificent creations as one might hold a rat by the tail, thus announcing myself as a greenhorn or a philistine or both – there is such a thing as *face*; (ii) in any case, some of the fruit come without a stalk – if you have to handle some, you might as well handle them all; (iii) finally, you have to grip them if you are to shake them properly – I'll explain this bit later.

So there I'd be, pawing the produce without ever a wince or a curse and bringing into play a store of expertise accumulated over several durian seasons, bent on convincing my audience that I was capable of selecting only those durians that were in peak condition. One golden evening down by the river when I was on my haunches inspecting the fragrant specimens, I heard a youthful voice above my head, a voice charged with scorn:

"Europeans do not like durian."

I had been told this many times over the years. I had also been told that durian was 'heaty' and that to eat it while drinking beer was dangerous and might even be fatal. Yet I had eaten scores of durians, and washed a good many down with Singha Beer in Thailand and Tiger Beer in Singapore and Malaysia. The lad's statement too was a crude generalisation, so this time I straightened up and gave him a crude, but truthful, reply: "I was eating durians before you were born."

"Dat velly good answer," said a diminutive old Chinese lady whose presence I hadn't been aware of, and we smiled at each other while the youth melted into the dusk.

If you haven't been put off already, you may be wondering *how* one picks out a good durian. I'm not sure that I can help you; but since everyone in Sarawak seemed to have a personal set of guidelines that didn't quite coincide with anyone else's, I suppose that I might as well give you my own checklist, amateur though I am. I apologise to any reader who is so expert that he has not for many a year bought (forgive the phrase) a bum durian. To the others, I must stress that the whole business of trying and buying is a matter of some gravity and that if you carry this off well your social standing will be greatly enhanced, even if what you carry off home is inedible. Here, then, is my own set of seven 'S-tests' for a durian:

> **SMELL**: Hold it well away from the rest and sniff it well. If it doesn't make your mouth water, reject it even if the results of the following tests are positive.
>
> **STEM**: Hold the fruit cupped in one hand and scrape your thumbnail across the top of the stalk, where it parted from the tree. If it isn't sappy but is dry or even fibrous, reject it as not fresh enough.
>
> **SIGHT**: Probably the best colour is bronzy-green, though some yellowish ones can be good if not yet breaking open. Since wild creatures are good judges, fruit with holes made by monkeys or insects are (or at least were once) good. Do not dismiss them; just bargain the price down.
>
> **SIZE**: I favour smallish spherical specimens rather than large irregularly-shaped ones...
>
> **SHAPE**: ...but I have heard locals praising those shaped like an

elongated egg.

SPINES: These should all be firm, sharp and new-looking except perhaps for the patch that hit the ground when the fruit fell and is matted with leaf-mould. But beware: some unscrupulous vendors pick unripe fruits and *throw* them on to the ground. Some locals also swear by fruit that have closely-packed spines, but I haven't noticed that they're any better than the rest.

SPECIFIC GRAVITY: If a fruit seems a bit light for its size I find it augurs well, because lighter fruits tend to have a greater flesh-to-husk ratio.

SOUND: Without wincing or grimacing, grasp your fruit as firmly as you can with one hand at the top and the other at the bottom. Raise it towards your ear so that the stem is horizontal and shake it vigorously from side to side. The delicious rows of pulp covering the seeds should wobble a little; you may not be able to hear this, but you should be able to feel it.

It was in 1959 near Bangkok that I bought and tasted my first durian (*Durio zibethinus*, by the way). Although I was not disgusted by it, I was unimpressed and made the mistake of leaving the rest overnight in the fridge, which the following morning had to be switched off, emptied out, washed thoroughly and left open for half a day. Even so, everything in the fridge smelt of durian for days. Perhaps that was how I came first to accept and then to appreciate the aroma and so became known to a small circle of friends as a durian expert.

The last ones I bought before leaving Sarawak in 1982 were a couple that I selected very carefully from a riverside vendor in Kuching. Why both of them turned out to be duds I can't imagine.

10: GOING TO WORK IN MANDALAY

On my first day of work at the university I came out of the Mandalay Hotel grounds and greeted a circle of fellows squatting in the shade and playing some sort of board-game on the paving-stones.

"Mingala-ba!"

"Mingala-ba, hsaya!" they replied with broad grins, thus signifying (teachers merit the appellation 'hsaya') that they already knew I was the new lecturer at the university.

I was ushered round the corner towards the horse-carts, but I wanted the cheaper saiq-ka, the Burmese trishaw. There was just one, parked in the shade of a flame-of-the-forest tree. The driver asked for twenty kyat and came down to ten. In my fragments of Burmese and his rather larger bits of English we chatted as he pedalled me to work. I couldn't persuade him that "saiq-ka" was borrowed from the English "side-car". He was convinced that it was the other way round, since this type of pedicab was a Burmese invention. I knew he wasn't right about the word, but he might well have been right about the invention itself. A certain Major Raven-Hart, who had visited Mandalay shortly before World War II, had written of 'a curious vehicle invented I believe here... a cycle, not a motor-cycle, with a diminutive side-car into which two people can fold themselves: there is about as much room for each as in a doll's perambulator.'

The two seats faced fore and aft. I wedged myself into the forward-facing one. The leisurely twenty-minute ride to the university was pleasant, January being cool and sunny. Groups of young children dressed in green and white were toddling off to school. Their teachers, each dressed in a white blouse and a green longyi, a sort of ankle-length sarong, sedately pedalled along on their bicycles or elegantly sat side-saddle behind a husband. Ancient small-nosed buses full to overflowing, with a few men clinging onto the side doors and a dozen onto the back, trundled slowly past knots of cyclists and stopped to pick up yet more passengers, only to be overtaken by the cyclists.

The tenor of town traffic was gentle. Apart from an occasional modern Japanese pick-up careening under a load of people and goods and brassily demanding its way through the throng, there was just the creaking and clicking of slowly-pedalled bicycles, the chatter and laughter of those pedalling and rumble of the occasional old dilapidated 'line bus'. Turning south on 73rd Street, we joined a broad river of bicycles and saiq-ka all heading towards the university, where lectures were due to start in a few minutes. This southbound traffic occupied the whole road; the few motor vehicles heading north had to weave from one side to the other, nosing their way slowly against the stream.

Not far from the university gates, sitting back from the road on a patch of wasteland, was the emblematic and slightly disturbing figure of a paper-buyer, sitting behind a low wooden table. He bought all kinds of re-usable paper; today his table was laden with bundles of used exercise-books. Before him hung the two large pans of his weighing-scales which flashed in the morning light and gave his dark face an intermittent luminosity. The scales were suspended from what can only be described as a little gibbet, to the top of which a sinister bunch of dead flowers was tied as if to mourn the death of knowledge. The university students' used exercise books seemed to be his main stock-in-trade. Weeks, months, years of learning were weighed in great bundles and found to be worth a few pya, the price of a small glass of sugar-cane juice. The paper was sold and put to good use. For example, I had bought some local grapes in a paper bag made from a student's English language exercise book. It read:

1. I do not play. He does not play. (or) I do not play, nor does he.
2. He did not go. I did not go. (or) Neither he nor I went.

And so on. In my imagination, this paper-buyer was The Final Marker, sitting in judgement outside the university, pronouncing Education meaningless and Qualifications hardly worth the paper they were written on.

By mid-March the heat had got too uncomfortable for side-car rides, so I had started going to work by horse-cart. In the mornings the little horses cropped what little withered grass there was as they waited around the corner from the hotel in the thin shafts of shade of a roadside tree. The drivers had worked out a rota so that the fares would be evenly spread. As I approached, one of them would give his gaunt horse a bag of greyish chopped hay and greet me with a bright smile and a cheery 'Mingala-ba, hsaya'. By now they knew where to take me and how much I was – and was not – prepared to pay; so I could jump in without having to bargain.

The Mandalay horse-cart, or myin-hleh, which some of the older folk called a 'gharry' when speaking English, was a two-wheeled trap on leaf-springs with a low-sided body and an arched roof of four or five iron ribs, covered with a fitted canopy of plastic material. The body and wheels were brightly painted red, yellow, blue and green and the canopy was trimmed in similar colours and decorated with appliqué floral and geometric shapes. The registration number was brightly painted too: the drivers of myin-hleh 999 and 1234 were particularly proud of their numbers and had painted them with special care. The cartwheels were shod with car-tyre rubber and each had an eyebrow-shaped mudguard of wood or, occasionally, brass. Some carts bore old coach-lamps, which I never saw lit even on the darkest nights.

On these morning rides I would step into the cart by the tiny rear door and settle down on a side bench just behind and to one side of the driver, so that I could see the way ahead. I did this because the scalloped hem of the canopy reached down below shoulder-level and blocked the side view. Above the hem in one cart there were one or two heart-shaped mirrors sewn into the canopy. These were presumably for any lady who wished to see if her spray of 'Dancing Ladies' – small, delicate yellow orchids – was still in place in her chignon, or any girl who wanted to check that the powdery thanahka leaf-shapes on her cheeks were as yet unsmudged. As my cart lurched into motion, I would brace myself against the rhythmic farting – the horse's, of course – that accompanied the sprightly hoof beat. When that was over, I could enjoy the coolness of a trotting-speed breeze in the shade of the canopy.

The condition of the horse usually contrasted sadly with that of the gaily-painted cart. Most of the poor creatures seemed underfed and overworked and, as the long hot day wore on, they wearied. The weather was now uncomfortably hot even in the shade, and my home-ward journeys were quite different from the morning trips. By four o'clock the streets had melted and black boils had appeared under a skin of pale dust. The clip-clop of hoofs was muffled as the horseshoes branded the molten tar with deep glistening scars, and the road hissed like Sellotape as it unstuck itself from the wheels. After a kilometre or so, the driver's head would loll, the horse's head would go down, the pace would slacken to a walk and I would begin to sweat even more profusely in the absence of breeze. I didn't mind this and was never in a hurry, but the driver would rouse himself and whack the bony haunches to push the poor animal into a trot again through the sweltering town.

Mandalay's flat grid of dusty unkempt streets seems always to have been a disappointment to visitors for whom the town's name had Kiplingesque resonances; but there was always something interesting to see if you watched what people were doing. One of the simple everyday sights I had become fond of was the sugarcane crushers at work. Leaning against a large shady tree there would be a few dozen very tall sugarcanes and nearby a stack cut into half-metre lengths. A squatting figure would strip the green skin off these and place the succulent sticks of pith in a large bowl by the crushing machine. This was similar to one of those old-fangled mangles that used to squeeze water out of our laundry, but with these crushing machines you rotated the handle vigorously so that the shiny metal rollers turned and were kept in motion for some time by a large vertical flywheel, a weighty affair often painted kingfisher blue but with spokes of various pastel colours. Along 73rd Street and by Mingala market these large technicolour wheels spun prettily, squeezing out a refreshing drink which did not – as many bottled confections did – leave the drinker thirstier than before, and which cost far less.

The horse slowly zigzagging its way through the now sizzling town was no longer subject to morning flatulence, but a different hazard took its place. Slung just below the horse's tail was a hessian dung-bag which was occasionally emptied into the street; but of course quite a lot adhered to the bag and quickly dried off. Now, even when a horse is trotting, a persistent fly can tickle or sting in a sensitive spot and cause the tail to swish sharply. This flourish would sweep remnants of dung into the slipstream, on to my face, into my hair and over my clothing. For some time I had thought I was being blinded by dust and chaff raised by a passing breeze or vehicle, but when I discovered the true cause I decided that on my homeward trips I should sit in the rear with my back to the horse.

Almost everything took an extraordinarily long time to arrange in Burma. Having been appointed in Britain in October 1986, given the go-ahead by the Burmese authorities in December and arrived in January '87, I was still living in a hotel and had to wait until June for my little white Suzuki jeep to arrive. At about the same time I was able to move into a house of my own choosing, so henceforth I was not dependent on the hotel for accommodation or on the saiq-ka or myin-hleh to get me to work. It was at this point, I realise in retrospect, that I stopped learning Burmese. No longer did I interact with drivers and pedallers whose own English was nearly as bad as my Burmese. I had been prepared to make hilarious mistakes with those carefree fellows waiting for me outside the Mandalay Hotel and therefore learnt a great deal. Now I was alone, insulated in my smart white jeep, which took such a lot of manoeuvring through the river of cyclists that I arrived no sooner than if I'd taken a saiq-ka.

I always drove very carefully to the university, my motto being, 'There is nothing around a Mandalay cyclist'. That certainly suggests how they behaved: without a backward glance they would suddenly steer into the middle of the road to avoid a puddle or pothole; stop or turn in any direction without warning; and sail across a major road without pausing to check what traffic might be coming from left or right. One morning, having safely negotiated such hazards, I pulled up proudly outside the Department of English in my newly-arrived jeep. Lifting out my briefcase, I carefully locked the car door and turned purposefully towards the doorway. Then everything literally went black. I had walked slap-bang into the side of a large black cow that was passing. I managed to stay on my feet, but on looking around I saw a student grinning widely. I had lost face, and the story would get around fast. I had never before noticed how silently cows walk. The student untied his longyi, retied it and strolled away, still grinning. The cow sauntered into the grassy grounds around the Department of English, her velvety dewlap swaying like a theatre curtain that has just closed.

11: From elephants to ants

While driving my little white jeep to and from Mandalay University, I had at various times narrowly avoided all sorts of creatures: chickens and ducks, humans of various ages, dogs of several shapes and colours, pigs of all sizes from frisky pink youngsters to lengthy mud-covered sows, goats, bullocks and the great placid water-buffaloes that would occasionally lumber across the road, slow, single-minded and unstoppable. (I had long ago in Thailand learned that, when hit by a car, a buffalo will often just walk away leaving the vehicle badly damaged.) I thought that by now I had encountered all the jaywalkers that Mandalay had to offer, whether avian, human, canine, porcine, ungulate or otherwise. I was wrong.

Driving down 73rd Street towards the university's main gate one day I found myself, as I often did, behind a group of lads cycling slowly in line abreast, each with one arm on a neighbouring shoulder and all of them talking and laughing as they dawdled along taking up most of the street's width. In second gear I had just accelerated past them when I had to jam on the brake as hard as I could to avoid a disastrous collision. I had once again come almost face-to-face with an elephant. Fortunately there was just enough room to pull over and let the towering creature pass. As he walked by, the man leading the animal out of the campus gave me a look that left me in no doubt that he was questioning my sanity, and I realised what I had done. On overtaking the cyclists I had sounded a warning hoot which must have appeared to be intended for the elephant. Had I run into the beast and been squashed into a subsequent existence, I would like to think that some latter-day Orwell would have written my obituary and entitled it *Hooting an Elephant*.

Summer arrived, bringing temperatures well over 100° Fahrenheit. In the garden various birds were courting and nesting, the mangoes were fattening and some trees were shedding many of their leaves. In the cool of the early morning it felt as if spring, summer and autumn had arrived at the same time. The large turquoise blue lizards that had been dormant were now to be seen sunbathing on almost every tree trunk, either nodding vigorously or chasing dowdy little brown females up and down and round about.

Other reptiles had reappeared too. I had seen a couple of vipers on the road, and the first domestic snake of the season surfaced at the water-tap in the back garden. Burma had (and probably still has) the highest incidence of death by snake-bite in the world. In the Mandalay area, nine out of ten snake-bites were inflicted by Russell's Viper, one of the world's more deadly serpents. This creature and the cobra were common enough in the area to warrant caution when I was visiting old pagodas, whose sun-warmed bricks and cool crevices provided near-perfect living conditions for reptiles. Also common (though not in the city) was the python, which is non-venomous and kills by constriction. It grows to a considerable size and over the years has made quite a name for itself in Burma. Back in 1927, a twenty-foot specimen swallowed a sleeping hunter whole, feet first. The poor fellow had taken off his boots and stretched himself out under a tree; when the boots were found, the snake was discovered nearby in a state of post-prandial torpor and killed. An eight-year-old boy was eaten by a python of similar proportions in 1972.

Another reptile that emerged was what the Burmese call taukteh – the tucktoo, a heavily-built lizard that inhabits trees, roofs and verandahs. I preferred the more onomatopoeic Thai name, which sounds like 'took-eh'. The name comes from the series of hiccups-cum-belches the creature produces from time to time, most noticeably at night. It warms up with a short crescendo of single syllables (took-took-Took-Took-TOOK-TOOK) and then stops this stuttering to announce itself as 'TOOK-EH! TOOK-EH!' for anything up to a dozen times in a slow decrescendo. For some reason, the tucktoo is generally disliked in Burma and Thailand. Back in the '60s, my Thai colleagues had told me that once one of these lizards got your finger in its mouth you'd be unable to get it out without killing the thing and cutting its jaws away. They didn't tell me how or why anyone might contrive to get a finger stuffed down its throat in the first place.

The tucktoo's lesser cousin, a small house-gecko called ein-myaung ('house-dependant' is a rough translation) was what I had known in Thailand as 'chingchook' and in Sarawak as 'chichak'. No room in South-east Asia is complete without a dozen or so of these semi-translucent putty-coloured lizards. They scurry up walls and across ceilings – especially near lights, where insects gather – and snap up, often audibly, the mosquitoes, flies, beetles and other insects that have flown indoors. These little lizards will tackle almost any insect except ants and certain species of beetle. Being indoor creatures they do not hibernate during the cool weather.

At any time of year they may fall on you as you open a screen door or draw a curtain, whereupon you feel a brief cold wriggle like a weak electric shock, hear a faint 'splat' on the teak floorboards and look down to see a dazed little thing that you feel sure must be badly injured. But as you look, it scuttles across the floor, leaps on to the skirting-board and climbs up the wall to hide behind a picture or piece of furniture to nurse its pride, and perhaps a headache. Occasionally you wake up to find that in your sleep you have rolled over and squashed one. Sometimes you inadvertently crush one between door and jamb, and once, as I went to the ancient fridge and opened the door of the freezer compartment, I startled a young ein-myaung which leapt into the icebox and quick-froze itself. But on the whole the little creature could hardly count *Homo sapiens* as a natural enemy. True, those that inhabited my room at the university were a nuisance, in that every morning I had to brush their droppings off my books and papers; but as an insect-eater it was an ally, albeit one that was subject to occasional 'friendly fire'.

I don't much mind snakes and other reptiles, though of course you have to be wary of snakes because – unless you're an expert – it's often impossible to tell whether a particular specimen is harmless or deadly. For this reason a lot of harmless and even quite useful snakes are killed all the time. But whether venomous or not, snakes don't make my blood run cold, nor do insects. Large spiders, however, do.

I went down the garden one morning to inspect the well that supplied the house with water. Lifting the corrugated iron cover, I could see nothing at first but the reflection of a bright sky and some motionless palm-fronds behind the silhouette of my head. Then there was a movement of a point of light on the brick-lined wall of the well, just a foot or so from my right eye. Refocusing, I found that a huge spider was watching me. Two of its eyes glittered, taking in the sudden foreign light and refracting it like tiny shattered windscreens. I was being eyed with circumspect efficiency by a born killer standing much too close for my liking. The colour of dark soil, it had the squat body and powerful legs of a small crab. And the thing was bristly. Carefully withdrawing my head, I gently straightened and lowered the cover. Only then did I allow myself to breathe again.

Fortunately spiders weren't often a problem, but scorpions were. I once narrowly missed scooping up with my bare hands a large dark one that had taken up residence under some emptied-out packing material. On being discovered, it scuttled straight towards my bare foot; I first executed a standing leap towards the broom I'd been using, then executed the creature by using the broom as a sledgehammer. Sweating, I swept the bits outside. I always sweat when I have to kill anything much larger than a bluebottle.

On another occasion, I was about to use the downstairs toilet when I saw a pair of pincers sticking out of a small hole at the foot of the wall. As I had very recently seen a small land-crab scuttling away from the house and down the driveway, I thought this must be another and got down on all fours to have a closer look. The claws were too slender, too black; it was a large scorpion, ebony claws held akimbo, dead still.

Once again my face was too close for comfort. I backed away and called the gardener, who ran off and returned with one of my best carving-knives, positioned the blade flat against the wall and brought it down hard like a guillotine. The black pincers clicked into life and started working like some netherworld mechanical digger. As the gardener dragged the knife away from the wall, other sets of legs emerged, radiating from a squat black body. Finally the tail whipped upwards out of the crevice, and the venomous sting struck the blade. After a while the raised tail uncurled and slowly fell flat to the floor. It wasn't the biggest scorpion I'd seen – that had been one I'd come across in a Borneo forest – but it was the blackest. The gardener carried it away on the carving-knife, and before using the toilet I made sure the scorpion's mate wasn't nursing revenge anywhere nearby.

But as usual in the tropics, it was the smallest creatures that did the most damage. Of all the species of ants Mandalay could boast of, the second most annoying were the dark normal-sized ones that ran like the wind; the worst were the minute reddish ones that bit like tigers. Close-packed hordes of these little devils had already succeeded in achieving all the usual feats – invading the kitchen, colonising cupboards and either committing mass suicide in pots of jam sealed tight with screw-top lids or drowning in an alcoholic stupor in the dregs of wine, beer and spirits. Then for a fortnight or so they disappeared. Had they moved on? Was the ant season over? No. One morning when I couldn't get my radio cassette recorder to work, I lifted it up and found underneath it a heap of black dust. The little red devils had pulverised the cassette-to-cassette recording mechanism. But where were they now?

I soon found out.

The really hot weather had arrived, and the red ant High Command had decided that an air-conditioned bedroom was preferable to a sweltering kitchen. Under cover of darkness, patrols and search parties were sent out into the bedclothes. Encountering vigorous resistance and chemical warfare, they retired to regroup elsewhere. The new rendezvous turned out to be my study. Here they discovered huge reserves of edible glue in book-spines, lampshades and furniture joints. When one evening they took to climbing up the chair I was sitting on and marching into my shorts armed to the mandibles with formic acid, I retired for a drink. I found their dark, fleet-footed cousins living very comfortably downstairs in the ancient, dying refrigerator.

12: Eight, eight, eighty-eight

"Ready?... OK. Let's start."

It was 1990 and I was giving my postgraduate class in Manchester, most of whom were from overseas, a short quiz as a warm-up exercise.

"Number one. In 1988 thousands of people peacefully demanding democratic rule were slaughtered by their own government security forces when armoured vehicles and troops appeared on the streets of the city. In which capital city did this happen?"

All the students quickly and confidently wrote down their answers to this and to the rest of the questions.

"Right, let's check your answers. Number one. Yes, Mohamed?"

"Beijing."

"No, sorry. Anyone got a different answer?"

Nobody had. The students exchanged indignant glances and started muttering.

"It must be Beijing!" said one.

"I've got Beijing too!" said another.

"So have I!"

I settled the class down and explained. "No, that was almost a year later. The correct answer is: Rangoon."

Several of the students clearly didn't even know where Rangoon was. It was perhaps an unfair question. Because of the presence of television cameras in Tienanmen Square, the world had been able to see what happened there in 1989, but very few people knew anything about the far bloodier events that had taken place in Burma some months earlier. Perhaps I would have been equally unaware had I not been teaching in Burma at the time.

It's possible that Chinese culture had played some part in what happened. The Chinese calendar year has twelve moons, and there is a twelve-year cycle – the year of the rat, then of the ox, the tiger and so on, each year carrying a certain prognostication. An extra month is added to each twelve-year cycle to make up for lost time, as it were; and this extra month adds another element to the significance of that twelfth year. For example, every five cycles (i.e., sixty years) the year of the horse comes around 'with fire', and any girl baby born in one of these years will prove to be of a dangerous disposition and therefore virtually unmarriageable. The last time this year came around was in 1966, a year in which the birth rate in Taiwan fell by about 25% and countless women on the mainland had abortions. To bear a girl was bad enough; the thought of bearing an unmarriageable one was too much.

By contrast, 1988 was a year of the dragon. Boy babies born in such a year are sure to grow strong in body and mind and be lucky. Moreover, a double eight is the symbol of double happiness. It was hardly surprising, then, that in East and Southeast Asia many ethnic Chinese women strove to bear a son not merely in that year but precisely on the eighth of August (8-8-88), if necessary by Caesarian.

I cannot say how far the events in Burma at that time were influenced by the population's sizeable ethnic Chinese admixture – possibly not a great deal, because the Burmese themselves maintain an enduring faith in numerology. Whatever the case, nationwide unrest started simmering in the middle of 1988 when I was teaching at the University of

Mandalay. Disgusted with the ineptness of General Ne Win's totalitarian regime and the brutality of his so-called security forces, the population (including me) had now found their cash-in-hand wiped out overnight by the demonetisation of all the higher-value currency notes. By July the student movement in Rangoon was calling for a general strike, to begin on 8-8-88. This fact was reported on the BBC's Burmese and World services – nobody in Burma took any notice of the country's own news broadcasts – and with eager anticipation people were looking forward to the day when Burma would rise up like a great horse and throw off the government it had been saddled with for a quarter of a century. During those years the country, once the rice-bowl of the world, had steadily declined. From being one of the richest nations in Southeast Asia it had fallen to the status designated by the UN as 'Least Developed Nation'.

The Burmese are what westerners call superstitious, so it wasn't until the precise auspicious moment, eight minutes past eight on the eighth day of the eighth month, that the dockers in Rangoon downed tools and walked out. As news of this spread, people began marching in long orderly columns towards the city centre in a bid to achieve democracy and a respect for human rights. By sunset more than 100,000 people, with university students and monks taking the lead, had gathered in large groups at various spots in the city centre. The atmosphere was festive, the euphoria almost tangible. Then came the Bren-gun carriers and truckloads of armed troops. To this day nobody knows how many thousands were killed that night; but for days after, the demonstrations and killings went on, both in the capital and upcountry.

In Mandalay it took some time for me to piece together reliable details of the slaughter in the capital, but I didn't have to imagine the extent of the demonstrations. Every day huge numbers of men, women and children marched past my house peacefully and cheerfully between files of Buddhist monks, their chants and placards always making the same simple demands for human rights and democracy. In every street it was the same. The atmosphere in Mandalay was like that of a carnival; the sudden sense of solidarity was electrifying. People back home in England were just beginning to get interested in the approach of the year 2000 AD; but the people around me, who had been yearning for the arrival of 8-8-88 – the wonderful day when at last they would throw off the harness – were delirious.

Not so their government. Every school in the country had been closed by order; all university students had been sent home. The English Department staff room was therefore often deserted, though a handful of colleagues were helping me run an English course for the staff of several other departments, lecturers whose command of English was poor or at best very rusty. The course was going well, the glorious eighth day passed quietly and so did the next. But on the tenth only a few listless participants turned up. They brought news of a massacre that had occurred the previous day in the town of Sagaing, just a few miles downstream across the Irrawaddy river.

There was now little point in trying to continue the course. Rumours about the government-planned massacre were rife. The state-controlled press claimed that it had been necessary to fire into a mob attacking the police station and that thirty-one had died. This was a very different story from the one posted up in the information room established by the local students a few yards from my room in the English Department. It was not until another week had passed that, quite by chance, I was given an eyewitness account of what had really happened in Sagaing on that terrible Tuesday, the day *after* 8-8-88:

An Australian friend working nearby telephoned me at home.

"Burmese friend o' mine's been bitten by a rabid dog," he said. "Got any rabies vaccine?"

"Hold on."

I found some in the dying refrigerator.

"Yes, two doses. But it's pretty old stuff, and I – "

"Unactivated human strain?"

"Yes, that's what it says. But after all these power cuts we've had, I doubt if – "

"Great! Not to worry. Doctor says even if it's lost its effectiveness it won't do any actual harm. I'll send my mate round tomorrow morning first thing."

When the patient and his doctor arrived and I handed over the vaccine, the patient did not (as I would have done) rush off to have the first dose administered. He insisted on telling me his story in flawed but fluent English. He had witnessed the Sagaing massacre and was lucky to have escaped unharmed. He wanted me to tell the outside world what had happened, so here is a summary of what he said:

Hundreds of farmers had poured into Sagaing to join the demonstrations planned for 8-8-88. There was to be a massive march to Mandalay, but the security forces closed the bridge, the only one across the river, so that the town was unusually crowded. The unprovoked shooting of an unarmed man increased the resentment felt by the crowd, and on the following day – the ninth – they demonstrated noisily but peacefully outside the police station. At about three in the afternoon a single shot rang out; apparently this was a signal, because immediately there were bursts of automatic and single-shot gunfire from all around. A hail of bullets from a dozen or so vantage-points – roofs, upper windows, even trees – was poured into the crowded streets by armed men already in position. The slaughter went on and on. When the firing eventually stopped, an unknown number of people lay dead or wounded. Those still alive were finished off with rifle-butts and bayonets; many were then dragged to the riverbank and thrown in, others taken to the town mortuary. When this proved too small, rows of corpses were laid in an outside compound. Yet more bodies were dragged through a gap that the security forces cut through the barbed wire surrounding the police compound. These were distributed about the compound so as to make it look as if the police had been forced to fire in self-defence at an invading mob. That was the patient's story.

Two days later, he returned with his doctor and a third person to see if I had any further medical supplies. Now it was the doctor's turn to talk. He told me that he was on the run from the police because he knew too much about the massacre. He confirmed that the shooting had started at about 3 p.m. and described some of the casualties he had had to deal with. One bullet had hit his niece in the back of the head and burst her face open; another had hit a young man he knew low in the back and spilt his entrails. They were among the high number who had been shot from behind; there were still about a hundred of his patients in Sagaing, many of them still carrying a bullet that could not safely be removed. His equipment was limited and the conditions were unhygienic. After the very first wave of victims had poured in, for example, his staff had resorted to pulling down the dusty old curtains and tearing them into strips for use as bandages.

The third man then confirmed that a photographer had been ordered by the security forces to photograph the scene at the police station after the bodies had been dragged through the gap in the barbed wire. For the sake of verisimilitude, the doctor added, police officers had actually trodden on the bodies in order to make blood flow on the ground beneath them. If the machine-gun used by one soldier had not jammed, he said, the carnage would have been even greater.

I was unable to get copies of any official photographs except one of those taken in the mortuary compound, and this was later used in television programmes by Granada and the BBC. I did manage, however, to obtain a large crate of medical supplies from the British Embassy in Rangoon and tried, through various official avenues, to present this crate to the authorities. Since the government view was that no massacre had taken place, no medical supplies would be accepted. Two plain-clothes military intelligence men accosted me at the university, demanded to see the crate opened, interrogated me for a while and left.

No sooner had I managed to get the crate smuggled to a Sagaing hospital than the British Embassy decided that it was time to get out. They gave less than twenty-four hours' notice. Plane to Rangoon, where the Burmese were still demonstrating in magnificent defiance. Plane to Bangkok, where after some weeks of waiting it became clear that the people of Burma, having suffered tens of thousands of casualties, had failed to free themselves. Plane to Manchester, where I was able to supply BBC and Granada with the little evidence I had, give talks for Amnesty International and include Burma in my warm-up quizzes for my Masters in Education students.

A dozen years later, I still come across otherwise well-informed people who don't even know where Burma is, let alone what happened there in the eighth month of '88. And one thing still bothers me. Did that rabies patient survive, I wonder?

13: HERE AND THERE, NOW AND THEN: A POSTSCRIPT

In looking back over my forty years in the ELT profession, I suppose it's inevitable that what first comes to mind are the great changes that have taken place. Of all the 'now-and-then' contrasts, it's the technological advances that I find the most startling. For instance, when I began training teachers in Manchester in 1965, my newly-revised Shorter OED did not contain 'transistor', let alone 'byte', and 'RAM' was listed only as 'Royal Academy of Music'. Since then, all kinds of what we used to (but can no longer) call 'aids' have come and gone or changed almost beyond recognition, but I'll confine myself to one example: the language laboratory.

The memory of the first one I ever met still amazes me.

We're jumping back to 1959… I've parked my shabby black second-hand Standard Vanguard (it cost £80) between the Mercedes Benzes owned by other teachers at Patumwan College of Education, Bangkok. I climb to the first floor and turn into a sweltering room just big enough for the teacher's desk and 12 small cubicles. The windows are open of course; sparrows fly in and out, squabbling noisily and leaving deposits here and there. Only a dozen trainees are waiting for us, acting as guinea-pigs while I try to help a Thai teacher to use the state-of-the-art technology installed in the room. (Our usual classes are fifty strong.) At her desk the teacher doesn't address her students in the normal way; she feels obliged to use the microphone, so they receive their instructions through sweaty headsets. In front of each is a turntable with a reddish rubbery disc on it, a playing arm tipped with a steel needle, a microphone, an on-off switch and a rocker-switch. Oh, and a large eraser.

Each student lifts the playing arm, places the needle near the rim of the disc and waits. The teacher switches on at her desk and the disc revolves, recording a text that each student can hear through the headset. When the arm reaches the centre, the turn-table stops and the student lifts the arm off, replaces to the beginning, throws the rocker-switch and switches the turntable on again. Now is the time for the

75

student to listen to the scratchy recording and respond. The student's voice goes through the needle onto the disc until that stops, whereupon the arm is lifted off. When the arm is replaced and the rocker-switch is thrown back again, the student can start up once more and compare the original scratchy recording to the even scratchier responses. At the end of the session, all the discs are made to spin, and the students pick up their erasers and apply them so that they brush the grooves and literally wipe out the recordings. The discs are now ready for the next session.

Seen from the age of the computer, satellite TV and the World Wide Web, that piece of equipment had all the charm, and none of the usefulness, of a penny-farthing bicycle. But in 1959, to the college staff and students and to me, it symbolised Progress.

The other kind of contrast that springs to mind is a 'here-and-there' as well as a 'now-and-then' matter. Again I will describe just one example:

Back in the Manchester of 1965, my standard letters, timetables and lecture-notes were typed by secretaries onto waxed stencils and duplicated, any reusable stencils being wiped and stored. A decade or so later, we lecturers were wondering how on earth we had managed before the coming of the photocopier; and soon video-cassette recorders, overhead projectors and computers were also available for teaching purposes. But let us now jump ahead to the Burma of 1987, to the English Department of the University of Mandalay...

The department has no set books for undergraduate studies, no photocopier and no supply of paper for teaching purposes. It has no duplicator and in any case no secretary able to type in English. So let us go downtown to a little shop where a man sits at an ancient typewriter. A lady lecturer comes in, bringing a set of last year's BA English course handouts, the yellowing and fibrous foolscap sheets already going brittle. The sheets are gummed together in sets at the top left-hand corner, staplers being expensive and wasteful of metal. The man is asked to type the material out again because the original stencils, used for two years, are now useless. The lady then departs.

Once the stencils are typed and corrected, she comes back, checks them and goes off again. The man runs off thousands of copies of handouts; the lady comes back and checks a sample. The texts are a bit faint because ink is expensive, but the time-honoured exercises have a familiar, reassuring look, and all the lecturers know the answers to the questions. The lady pays the man with money already collected from the students for this purpose; she then hails the driver of a 'side-car', the Burmese bicycle-rickshaw, and secures the bundle of handouts on it. Hailing another, she accompanies the load back to the department, where her colleagues help her collate the sheets into little sets representing a term's work. The next day thousands of students descend upon the department to collect a copy.

I could go on for hours (indeed, I have often done so) about such 'normal' circumstances. In vast areas of the world, teachers have to operate in oppressive heat, lacking books and equipment and receiving their low pay irregularly; their students lack nourishment and general knowledge often have to use a foreign language as their medium of schooling; they have no electricity at home and so on. But instead of dwelling on that darker side of things I shall end with a selection of half a dozen scenes that remain bright in my memory.

Here they are, in date order:

1960. A teacher is absent, so I'm teaching a double class of about sixty Thai eleven-year-olds in a hot wooden L-shaped classroom where I have moved the blackboard into the angle so that the kids can all see my necessarily huge writing. Of course, when I go round one half of the class I can't see the other half, but the kids are well-behaved. Running the class is a sweaty business and I'm already exhausted, but I'm winning.

1972. I'm giving a demonstration class. My three dozen primary kids are sitting on the ground in the shade of a huge mango tree on the hill behind Makerere University.

1978. I'm having to write a reading text around a large shell-hole in the blackboard while giving a demonstration class in Hanoi.

1980. After four days journeying up the River Baram in Sarawak and sleeping on longhouse floors each night, I have to jump out of the longboat and help manhandle it over rocks and tree-roots – all in a day's work for the primary school inspectors I'm accompanying.

1986. I've driven the British Council Land Rover northwards from Bamenda through axle-deep mud and across a rocky hillside, and now I've got to go through this fast-running river if I'm to run my short course for up-country teachers in NW Cameroon.

1988. I've been wondering for some time whether my teaching in

Mandalay has been doing any good, and now in the middle of a lesson, I've become aware of a strange reverberation and creaking in the classroom. I turn round from my blackboard to find the classroom empty and the back wall of the room falling towards me. Before I can move, the lofty structure comes crashing down, raising a cloud of dust.

My students, being accustomed to earth tremors and having far quicker reflexes than mine, have slipped out without a word of alarm or warning. If they return to find me brained on the spot, well, that will have been my 'kan', my karma, the fate of an undeserving teacher. But the topmost timbers have thudded down just a yard in front of me, so maybe my teaching hasn't been so bad after all.

Gerry Abbott

Part II:
Bob Jordan

I was at school in London, like Gerry, but in Chiswick, in the west. I also did National Service, in the RAF, before going to university, serving in different parts of Britain as well as two weeks in Cyprus. To get there I went in a Beverley transport plane – my first experience of flying. In my diary at the end of the two years' service, I noted: 'a love of travel has developed'. This feeling was to grow in the years to come.

The following episodes range from my first ELT work abroad in 1961 immediately after I graduated, to 1982, when I had been teaching English for Academic Purposes at Manchester University for ten years. My first degree was in Economics from St John's College, Cambridge. It might be thought Economics is not the best background for English teaching, but I found it useful when conducting discussion groups for business people in Finland. I also found it invaluable when I started teaching at Manchester, as quite a number of the postgraduate students I taught were studying Economics. I was able to specialise in English for Economics and thus give them more help.

The British Council recruited me for an ELT position in Finland in 1961, where I stayed until 1963. The following year I joined the Council and, after being sent to the Institute of Education, London University, to study for a qualification in EFL (PGCE), I was posted to Nepal in 1965 for four years and to Sierra Leone in 1970 for one. In 1971 I left the Council; the following year I joined the Manchester University's ELT Unit, which had been founded by Ken James two years previously. We worked together harmoniously for the next twenty-one years, until I took early retirement in 1992. While at Manchester, I went abroad nearly every year on short courses for the Council, mostly in Europe and Asia. Such visits gave real meaning to the saying 'Variety is the spice of life'.

Working abroad had many interesting aspects and some of the most memorable have been selected for this book. I have described the incidents just as they happened, based on notes made at the time, in order to give a flavour of the situation and period.

Out of the twelve countries I taught in, my favourites were Finland and Nepal, as I lived in them for longer and got to know them better. If I think of Finland, I immediately conjure up memories of winter snow and cross-country skiing, lakes, islands and saunas, and listening to the music of Sibelius. When I recall Nepal, there are vivid memories of trekking among mountains and valleys, especially around the Annapurna and Everest regions, with their wonderful views. Living in a mixed Hindu and Buddhist culture, with all the colourful temples and shrines, was fascinating. A line from Rudyard Kipling's poem 'In the Neolithic Age' might sum it up:

"And the wildest dreams of Kew are the facts of Khatmandhu."

1: OFF THE BEATEN TRACK

What on earth was I doing in a small town in the extreme south-east of Finland, at the height of the Cold War? The abortive Bay of Pigs episode had taken place in April 1961 and was followed the next year by the Cuban missile crisis, leading to confrontation between the USA and USSR in October '62. Yet here was I in Lappeenranta, from the autumn of 1961 to the summer of '63, only about twelve miles from the Russian frontier.

At the end of my first year as a student at Cambridge, I had decided to do something unusual in my long vacation in 1959: to hitchhike through Belgium, Holland, Germany, Denmark and Sweden to Finland, to visit the country where my father had had a pen-friend in the 1920s. It took three weeks to cover the 2,000 or so miles and I arrived in early September. I felt how different the country was from the others I had travelled through. The vast expanses of forests and lakes gave an air of calm and solitude, and there were very few other foreigners around.

I was struck most of all by the strangeness of the language. On looking around the harbour town of Turku where I arrived and then Helsinki, I recognised only one word and that was on some cars – taksi. I guessed that the word 'pankki' on some buildings was 'bank', but I could find no resemblance between Finnish and any other European language I had come across for the numbers one to five: yksi, kaksi, kolme, neljä, viisi.

By chance I met a British teacher of English in Turku and discovered that, if you were a native English-speaker and had a degree from a British university, you could teach English as a foreign language to adults. A teaching qualification in EFL was not necessary in those days. You could apply through the British Council in London, which acted as recruitment agent for Finnish-British Societies in about thirty-five towns. These teaching posts had started soon after the Second World War as a way to help Finland make contact with Western Europe. I stored this away for future use and returned to England by a Russian liner, *S.S. Baltika*.

Early in my second year at university I met a Finn at the International Centre. Ulf had been sent by his employer to learn English at the Bell Language School in Cambridge. He was about ten years older than I was but we had a common interest in rowing. Our developing friendship confirmed my desire to teach in Finland for a year. So in my final year I applied for and obtained a teaching post. Soon after graduating I travelled to Helsinki with other English teachers on the same ship, *SS Baltika*, from Tilbury Docks. Being on a Russian ship at this time added some excitement to the journey, and talk with some of the teachers often turned to spying and wondering whether or not our cabins were bugged. We later found out that one of the British diplomats, travelling back to the Embassy in Helsinki with his family, had found a microphone inside his bedside lamp.

We arrived in Helsinki in September '61 and went to our various destinations. I went by steam train to the small town in the south-east, on the southern edge of the enormous Lake Saimaa in southern Karelia – Lappeenranta ('Shore of the Lapps'), or to give it its Swedish name, 'Villmanstrand' (Wild Man's Shore).

I was met at the station by the middle-aged chairman of the Finnish-British Society. Lars took me to my accommodation, a rented room in a flat owned by a nurse in the local hospital; on the way he told me a little about the town. There were about 22,000 people, mostly Finnish-speaking but with some Swedish speakers. Apart from one Italian who lived there with his Finnish wife and ran a restaurant, I was the only foreigner. Most people worked in the timber trade, as the whole area consisted of forests of pine and silver birch. When trees were felled to go to local wood, pulp or paper mills and factories, the trunks were linked together in rafts and pulled in their thousands by tugs across Lake Saimaa, the largest of the 187,000 lakes covering Finland.

Lars told me that the town's Finnish-British Society was one of the oldest in Finland, being founded in April 1946. Linking with the English Club of Kaukas, a nearby timber firm, it recruited its first English teacher through the Council in September '49. Although the Society still appointed the teachers, from 1953 Saimaan Kansalaisopisto, the adult evening institute, took over the payment of the salary and the arrangement of lessons for members of the Society, Kaukas English Club and other groups – mainly employees of a cement factory and a wood pulp factory, as well as some housewives. Contracts were for one year, but they could be extended to two, and half of the teachers since the inception of the programme had done so.

Lars asked me what I knew about Finland. I said that I had read my predecessor's report but really knew very little. I had read about the Winter War when Russia had invaded Karelia, the province in which I now lived, on 30th November 1939. The war had lasted 105 days and was fought in an especially harsh winter, with temperatures as low as -40°C. The Finns fought valiantly but were completely outnumbered by the Red Army. The Finnish army did have some advantages which helped to delay the Russian advance: they wore white camouflage and skied through the forests, something the Red Army could not do. Although the Finns had practically no anti-tank artillery, they improvised with bottles of petrol and oil with TNT charges that they threw at tanks: these became known as 'Molotov cocktails'. I had also heard of Field Marshal Mannerheim, leader of the Finnish army and president of the republic for two years after the war.

Another name that I knew was Paavo Nurmi – 'the flying Finn' – the most famous of long-distance runners, who had won nine gold medals in three Olympic Games in the 1920s. On a lighter note I said that I was also aware of the three S's – Sibelius (particularly for *Finlandia*), snow (for cross-country skiing) and sauna (for cleansing all parts of the body). A little later, when I had learned some Finnish, I added to this list – 'Suomi' (Finnish for Finland) and 'sisu' – a special word that combines guts, stamina, resilience and determination, certainly qualities displayed by Finns in the war.

The day after I arrived, I was taken to the institute near the town centre where many of the evening classes were to be held. The well-built director, Kalevi Korhonen, outlined my teaching programme, to begin the following week. Most of the classes would be in the evenings, Monday to Friday: the busiest evening was to be Monday, from 5 p.m. to 10 p.m.. A few afternoon classes would be with the employees of wood pulp and cement firms and, as an extra, some in the local girls' grammar school. In addition to my thirty classes a week, there would be two club evenings a month, at a weekend, one with the Society and one at Kaukas. I would have to organise entertaining activities. I wondered what I would do with all my free time!

I needn't have worried: I still managed to write a weekly article in English for the local paper, *Karjala*. This provided reading practice for all my students.

That evening I went to a local restaurant as guest of some of the Society's committee members. Introductions were always formal, with people standing erect and shaking hands with head slightly bowed. In the restaurant I observed that whenever soldiers in their grey uniforms came to the doorway, they stood smartly to attention and saluted before walking in. There was a general air of formality in initial contacts with people. Most men and women wore hats, and men always raised theirs to each other on meeting.

The dinner was memorable. It was the first time I had ever heard of, or eaten, beef Stroganoff, named after a 19th century Russian diplomat. There was also reindeer meat on the menu, something I had never seen before. Dark rye bread accompanied most meals. I soon learned the Finnish for 'beer' – olut – and how to say 'cheers' – kippis. I noted that the reserve and formality dropped away as more beer or whisky was drunk.

The next morning I was at the institute, where Kalevi had arranged a press reception for me to be interviewed, in order to promote the English classes in the local newspapers. He said he would act as interpreter if the reporters did not have enough English. Three reporters greeted me in turn; I was now prepared for the formality. The first reporter brought his heels together, stood to attention and extended his hand. "Päivää," he said, bowing his head. I did likewise, or tried to. "Jordan", I said. The next man stiffened, held out his hand and, head slightly bowed, greeted me in a similar fashion. "Päivää", he said solemnly. "Jordan", I repeated, slowly realising that something was not quite right. By the end of the third friendly exchange I knew something was wrong. "Kalevi", I whispered. "Is 'Päivää' a common name here?" "No," he grinned. "'Hyvää päivää' means 'How do you do?' Informally it is shortened to 'päivää'." "Oh, Lord," I groaned, "I hope those reporters don't think 'Jordan' means 'päivää'." He laughed and said he would clear up any misunderstanding.

The following Monday my classes started with between ten and twenty adults to a class. The books to be used were inherited from my predecessor or were requested by the mature students. This was just as well as it was my first experience of teaching EFL abroad, only having done it for a few weeks in the summer at The Studio School of English, a private language school in Cambridge.

I couldn't believe my eyes when I saw a book for a group of beginners. It was published in Helsinki and had useful grammatical explanations and lists of vocabulary translated. The title *English with Bob* could not have been more appropriate! I wondered what the reactions would be to 'Lesson Seven: Rules for Pupils':

> What a Pupil Must Do. He must sit still in class. He must listen to the teacher. He must answer loudly. He must be polite. He must do his home-work. It is difficult to remember these rules and it is hard to keep them.

I also wondered what the women in the group would think, especially as I had discovered that Finnish does not distinguish between male and female in its pronouns: 'hän' is 'he' or 'she'. Perhaps they would assume that the rules were only for males.

Flicking through the book I paused at 'Lesson Sixteen: Strange Tennis-Balls'. I wondered if I would be able to keep a straight face when we came to read some of the dialogue:

"Bob, our balls have disappeared... Has Bob seen the balls?... What does Bob say about the balls?"

I imagined what I might be tempted to say!

Other books I would have to use were standard at the time, especially *Essential English for Foreign Students* by Eckersley and *Living English Structure* by Stannard Allen.

Settling into my teaching, I noticed one trait that was fairly common among students. The younger ones did not like to speak unless they were sure that what they said was grammatically correct. I often had to prompt them to speak with direct questions. In addition, some of the more elderly students did not want to change groups or move to a more advanced class once they had got used to the course book and felt comfortable with it. This was particularly so for one retired doctor who had been in the same intermediate group for three years. He liked the book he was using, knew it almost by heart and always knew the answers to any questions.

After a while, I became aware that most of the people I taught had a good sense of humour and enjoyed a laugh. By deliberately feeding some amusing questions, answers or comments into the exercises in the books, I helped to lighten the teaching and learning load. This created its own problem: sometimes students were not sure if I was serious or joking. I soon found the solution: I made two flashcards out of plain postcards and kept them in my pocket. On one I wrote 'JOKE' and on the other 'SERIOUS'. If ever the students were in doubt I simply held up the appropriate card.

'Serious' was also an appropriate word to describe my rather unsuccessful attempts to learn Finnish. The totally different grammatical structure of the language caused most of the problems: each noun had fifteen case endings and fifteen plural forms. Combined with this was the need to make additional changes to letters or syllables because of the system of vowel harmony, meaning that only certain sounds could go with each other. There are no articles or prepositions:

instead suffixes are used. For example, 'to Helsinki' is Helsinkiin, 'from Helsinki' is Helsingistä and 'in Helsinki' is Helsingissä. It was imperative to get the right ending when trying to book train tickets.

One morning, going into a local greengrocer's and wishing to practise my Finnish, I asked for "puoli kilo" – half a kilogram of "ripuli" – "grapes" as I thought. The young woman serving stared at me, backed away, turned around and ran to the back of the shop calling to someone.

A middle-aged man appeared, came towards me, and gruffly asked "Mitä?" – "What?" I repeated my request. He also stared at me, frowning. I thought it was time to start indicating the grapes that I wanted. I pointed at them and again said, slowly and clearly, "puoli kilo ripuli", and added "olkaa hyvä" – "please".

He looked at me, looked at the grapes, repeated slowly what I had said and suddenly roared with laughter. He called out to the young woman: she joined him at the counter. He explained something to her in rapid Finnish, and they both laughed loudly.

By now I was feeling uncomfortable. Why were they laughing? I simply pointed again at the grapes and asked for "puoli kilo". This time I was successful in getting what I wanted.

Later that day I asked Lars, whose English was good, the reason for the laughter. Was it just my funny accent? I repeated exactly what I had said. He also laughed uncontrollably. Eventually he was able to say:

"In Finnish, 'grape' is rypäle and you said ripuli. Can you hear the difference?"

"Yes", I said, and asked hurriedly, "What does ripuli mean?"

"Diarrhoea", he exclaimed.

"Oh my God", I muttered, shrinking with embarrassment! No wonder the woman had called for help. – I avoided that shop for some time.

As snow is on the ground in Finland for four to five months of the year, it looms large in people's lives. Thus it is not surprising that numerous words describe its condition and the different types. In fact, there are about 300 words for snow in Finnish and its dialects. The differences can be slight, but they are relevant to people for whom cross-country skiing is a necessary way of life. For example, vitilumi is 'new, freshly fallen snow' and nuoskalumi is 'wet, melting snow'. As well as all the words for snow, a number of words describe ski tracks, combined with adjectives to indicate their condition – soft, hard worn, slippery etc.

Snow usually started falling in November, with temperatures often dropping to -20 to -30°C or even lower during the following weeks. It could be so cold that, if I had a runny nose, an icicle would form which I would snap off when it reached my upper lip. To keep warm, several layers of clothing were needed and a fur hat.

In this world of snow and ice it became essential to learn to ski – cross-country style with long, narrow wooden skis. The main streets were regularly cleared by snowploughs, creating banks of snow several feet high in the gutters, acting as barriers between the pavements and roads. Outside the town centre the only way to get around was on skis.

Finns learn to ski soon after they can walk and run, so that by the time they start primary school at age six they are fairly proficient. It was a strange sight for many to see an adult getting his skis crossed, losing his balance and constantly falling over. I felt sympathy for zoo animals as groups of children gathered round to watch my early attempts, pointing and laughing as I floundered in the snow.

After several weeks of daily effort, I became sufficiently competent to join friends on their weekend ski outings. These started by meeting at the road which led out of the town, then following ski tracks down through the pine trees to the edge of the lake. The view was of flat whiteness, with snow-covered trees all around and on the islands in the lake, which by January had frozen over with very thick ice and two or three feet of snow on top. I was amazed at the uses which the frozen lake was put to. Snowploughs cleared a road across it from town to the outlying villages, and soon single-decker buses were following a regular route over the ice. At first I was apprehensive about travelling on these, imagining the worst possible scenario of cracking ice and freezing water. However, I changed my mind when I was shown an account of the Winter War, telling of Russia sending tanks across the frozen Baltic Sea.

The weekend ski tours in the few hours of winter daylight invariably followed tracks across to the islands lying a mile or so from shore. These tree-covered bits of land became hills, with tracks weaving between the pines and silver birches. Sometimes pairs of ski tracks went on both sides of a tree: in such cases it was crucial to keep your skis parallel and not allow them to diverge. The consequences could have been painful!

Skiing across the lake in February, I was surprised to see men sitting on stools next to holes they had managed to cut and chip in the deep ice. Into these they had dropped fishing lines and sometimes erected wooden tripods above them to let the lines hang while they skied around or plodded on snowshoes to keep warm. The fish they were after were quite large, either pike, perch or pike-perch, which tasted delicious when grilled over a pinewood fire.

A political joke, popular at the time, concerned Urho Kekkonen (1900-1986) who was Finland's longest serving president, from 1956 to 1981. He followed the pattern set by his predecessor, Paasikivi, in establishing a neutral position between Russia and the West – absolutely essential for Finland's survival, given its geographical position. This became known as the Paasikivi-Kekkonen line and involved walking a political tightrope.

The story goes that a youth was skiing across a frozen lake when he saw a man fishing over a hole in the ice. He paused to see if he had caught anything, then noticed that the fishing line had pulled taut. Suddenly it jerked, and the fisherman lost his balance and fell into the freezing water. The youth skied quickly to the hole, held out a ski pole for the man to grab and carefully helped him to climb back onto the ice. The freezing-wet figure hugged the youth – "Thank you, my boy, do you know whose life you have just saved?" The youth looked puzzled – "No, sir." The balding man smiled and said, "The President of Finland, Urho Kekkonen". The youth stared, looked shocked and said, "Please sir, don't tell my father" and quickly skied off.

After one weekend of skiing, I was invited to join some friends at their lakeside summer cottage. Many, if not most, families have some kind of summer house, usually made of wood, in the countryside or near the coast. Finns have a passion for solitude and escape to the forests, lakes and islands when they can. Close to the summer cottage there will usually be the family's sauna, again made of local timber. The traditional sauna consists of a stove heated by pine logs with hot stones on top, on which you throw water to create steam and increase the temperature. There are three slatted pine platforms to sit or lie on, after you have stripped of course. You start at the bottom and, as you grow used to the heat, gradually move up to the top level.

The sauna is more than simply a steam bath; it is part of the way of life – a place to relax in, meditate, chat to family and friends and feel at one with nature. I was introduced to customs that had evolved over centuries but were now condensed for me into an hour. I was shown how to throw water on the stones for the maximum effect and how to beat myself with a bunch of birch leaves in order to stimulate circulation. It also gave the skin a pleasant scent.

After ten minutes in the steam, with sweat running everywhere, it was time to move into a cold shower in the next cubicle and then back to the steam. One of the friends laughed and said, "This is better than water" and sprayed beer from a bottle onto the hot stones. The mildly alcoholic fumes made me feel light-headed, and without a moment's thought I joined the others in running outside into the deep snow and rolling stark naked in it – another old custom!

The final lakeside custom I would not have believed if I had not taken part in it. After another few minutes at the highest level in the sauna, again with sweat dripping from every pore, I was taken outside to a hole already cut in the ice at the edge of the lake. There, one at a time, we jumped in, staying for no more than twenty seconds, just long enough to shock the system, or strengthen the heart as the friends said, before running back inside for a final warm shower.

Many years later I only have to hear the music of Sibelius (1865-1957) to conjure up memories of the lake and forests. In particular his *Karelia Suite,* composed in 1893 for a pageant in Viipuri in southeastern Karelia and lost to Russia after the Winter War, never fails to stir me with its patriotic overtones and interplay of elemental powers. The coldness of the snow and ice is thawed by the warmth of the emotions aroused by the music.

2: Living with the Cold War

My first Christmas in Finland was spent as a guest of several families. I had the traditional lunch of lipeäkala – dried codfish softened by soaking it in an alkaline solution. This was quite a contrast to the English Christmas lunch I was used to. Irma, the nurse I was staying with, took me to visit some friends on Boxing Day on a horse and sleigh – another tradition and a lovely experience, listening to the horse's muffled hooves and the swishing of the runners on the icy snow.

Towards the end of December I joined a party of 73 mature American students and British teachers, all studying or working in Scandinavia and Finland, to go to Russia for eight days over the New Year. I thought it would be interesting to compare the two countries. Only two months before, on 30th October, the Soviet Union had test-exploded a 58 megaton nuclear bomb on Novaja Zemlja Island in the Barents Sea to the north-east of Finnish Lapland; two days prior to this, Finnish radio and newspapers had carried unprecedented warnings of precautions to take in the event of radioactive dust falling across Finland – when hearing sirens or radio alerts, "Cover the face with a gas mask, towel or gauze... Shut all windows, vents and doors... Shut yourself in a room with no outlets, e.g. sauna, bathroom or cellar..." My friends had explained all this to me and warned me to be ready for such an emergency. The reference to gas masks brought memories flooding back of infant school days in London in the '40s when I had to carry a gas mask to school every day. I prayed that such an eventuality would never happen.

On the same day that the nuclear bomb exploded, the USSR had delivered a Note to Finland in which there was a reference to "joint military consultations". One newspaper headline read "Finland Fears for her Neutrality". Immediately people were talking about the possibility of a Soviet invasion and the precautions to take. Fortunately, the matter was resolved at the end of November, but it brought home just how exposed and vulnerable people were in Finland in the intense Cold War.

Our train for the Russian trip started in Helsinki; I joined it on 29th December near Lappeenranta along with another English teacher named Malcolm who worked in Savonlinna, a beautiful mediaeval fortress town about sixty miles to the north-east. Before proceeding to Moscow we spent four days in Leningrad, including the New Year; there we saw models of Grandfather Frost (our Father Christmas). We stayed at the Hotel Europe, and Malcolm and I shared a twin-bedded room. A lot of talk at the time centred on the likelihood of our being bugged, and both of us guessed, correctly we think, that small microphones were hidden behind the fixed radiator grilles in our rooms. We had noticed the light reflecting off a different coloured piece of metal just out of reach and as a result were always careful about what we said.

After travelling all night by train from Leningrad, we arrived at the Hotel National, right in the centre of Moscow overlooking the Kremlin and Red Square. It was about 9.30 on the morning of 3rd January, snowing heavily, with the temperature about -15°C. Someone remarked "It'll be pretty hot here if the Cold War escalates". There were no laughs.

As we stood waiting for our rooms to be allocated, I felt one of the British teachers, Liz, touch my arm. In a startled but hushed voice, she said: "Look over there, quickly!"

I looked in the direction her eyes indicated across the crowded hotel foyer but noticed nothing unusual.

A few moments later, I felt her touch my arm again. She said urgently, "Did you see him do it?"

Now in a far corner I could see a tall man ostentatiously pulling his left ear lobe three times, pausing, then repeating the action.

"Do you think he can be one?" she asked, staring at me with a concerned look.

I looked at her with a smile. "A spy, do you mean?"

She nodded seriously.

Just then the man who had pulled his ear came over to us. Liz stood still. I broke the ice by saying,

"Liz, can I introduce John. He's from Ohio and studying in Helsinki. I'm surprised you haven't met before, especially as you're teaching there."

Liz looked first at John, then at me. John and I could not restrain ourselves any longer: we both burst out laughing. On the journey to Moscow, he and I had devised this practical joke. Earlier I had told Liz that a secret signal used between spies was to pull the lobe of the left ear three times in order to identify each other – rather like the handshake signal between Freemasons. John had played his part to perfection. Liz laughed.

"You really had me on," she spluttered.

Thoughts of spies and spying were pushed into the background during three days of intensive sight-seeing around Moscow. Led by the friendly and helpful Alexei, our trip covered the main tourist attractions – Red Square, Kremlin, St. Basil's Cathedral and the Bolshoi Theatre. We also visited GUM, Moscow's largest store and were intrigued to see an abacus being used to calculate costs. Walking around the streets, we were occasionally approached by small boys who asked us in broken English if we had any chewing gum or ball-point pens. Once as I walked briskly to keep warm, wearing my camel duffel coat, red scarf and brown fur hat, a youth walked by my side and asked if I would sell my shoes. I had to refuse. We had been warned about the dangers of selling things on the black market – apart from the fact that it would look odd walking around barefoot!

We returned to Red Square and joined the many thousands of Russians waiting patiently to see Lenin's body lying in the Mausoleum. As tourists, we were given a special concession to join the queue about 200 yards from the entrance, which was guarded by two sentries with bayonets fixed to their rifles. Inside, another eight sentries stood by the glass case containing Lenin, around which we slowly walked. The great Soviet Leader's frail face, with its thin moustache and little pointed beard, was clearly visible above the dark suit that covered him.

Later, back at the hotel, I asked Alexei why the only newspaper available in English in the stores or the hotel was the *Daily Worker*, the British Communist Party paper. His answer:

"Because it represents the workers in Britain".

"All the workers?" I continued.

"Yes," he confirmed.

"Why was the circulation in 1960 only 56,751," I persisted, "out of a working population of 24 million?" I had, of course, carefully prepared my information beforehand.

"Oh, it isn't a rich paper," Alexei smiled, and tried to pass off his response as the last word on the matter, adding that all the western newspapers were available in the Lenin Library, near the Hotel National, and anyone could read them there.

On our last evening in Moscow, John and I decided to conduct a small experiment. We felt it was our last chance to test the system, in this case to see which foreign newspapers really were accessible to Russian people. The more I thought about it, the more I began to have doubts – not about our ability to see it through, but about reactions from the Russians.

I kept my thoughts to myself, and after dinner in the hotel John and I armed ourselves with our passports and set off in the cold dark night, trudging the hundred yards through the snow to the library. We arrived just before 8 p.m., having checked earlier that it shut at 10 p.m.. We felt rather tired and a little nervous as we went to the young woman at the barrier, just inside the main door. By her side was an armed policeman. She did not speak any English but took us to a nearby office where another woman did.

We explained who we were and that we wanted to look at some American and English newspapers. She said we would have to become subscribers to the library, which took time. I responded that we were leaving Moscow that night and did not have time to wait for forms to be processed. We produced our passports to prove our identities.

The woman did not bother to look at them but picked up a phone, shielded the mouthpiece with her hand and spoke in Russian. John, who had kept quiet about his ability to speak Russian, was able to follow her brief conversation.

We then filled in a form, putting our name, nationality and profession. Another woman came in and asked us to follow her. She showed a security pass to the armed guard and took us along a passage, past another security check and into the magazine room. In it were a number of people reading papers and magazines. We were shown the catalogue in which all the British and American newspapers were listed. We filled in a form asking for the latest issues of *The Observer*, *The Guardian* and *The New York Times*.

Asked to wait, we sat at a nearby table by ourselves and looked around the room. It was then that John quietly told me of the telephone conversation at the entrance:

"She said, 'There are two men here: an Englishman and an American; they don't speak Russian. They want to look at English and American newspapers – be careful.'"

I glanced around at the other people. It was not at all clear who they were or what their status was. One thing was certain, however; after all the security checks involved and the need for permits, they were not the ordinary man or woman in the street.

I noticed that one man, sitting alone at a table in the corner, kept looking at us. I whispered this to John, adding:

"Why do you think they're taking so long? It's nearly twenty minutes. What are they up to?"

He slowly looked around and commented: "Maybe they're having difficulty finding the papers. Probably not many people ask for them."

I could not help wondering if there was a more sinister reason.

At last four copies of *The Observer* were brought to us: the latest dated 10th December, nearly a month before. Nothing appeared to have been cut from the pages; all had some kind of official stamp at the top. After another twenty minutes the other papers appeared. None were kept in the room itself: all had been sent for. The only English paper on view was the *Daily Worker*.

We only had a few more minutes left before we had to be back at the hotel for the return rail journey to Finland, so we hurriedly looked through some of the papers then handed them back. The man in the corner was still watching us. We were escorted to the cloakroom to get our coats and fur hats.

As we pulled our coats on, we said goodbye to the woman accompanying us. She swivelled as though to return to the reading room but when we had turned our backs, she also turned. We saw her run to the first office, perhaps to report our departure or to find out who we were. We felt a little frightened by the whole atmosphere, especially as we were sure we had been under constant surveillance.

John and I compared notes on our walk back to the hotel. We agreed that it had been an interesting experiment but not one that we would care to repeat. Convinced that we were being followed, every now and then we glanced over our shoulders, peering into the darkness. Apart from some elderly women sweeping and shovelling snow from the pavements, there didn't seem to be anyone else in sight. Then I spotted him – a black-coated policeman, some yards back, staying in the shadows: he seemed to be keeping pace with us.

I touched John's arm and whispered, "We *are* being followed."

John carefully peered over his shoulder and added: "I guess he's checking to see which hotel we go to."

As we entered the hotel, we saw him stop and then return the way he had come. At the end, he made no attempt to conceal himself: that was a warning in itself. Feeling rather anxious that he might come back with some comrades and take us away for questioning, we quickly told several of the group who were gathering in the foyer what had happened. The more people who knew about it the better. We had read of people "disappearing" in Russia and did not want to add to their number.

That night, Friday 5th January at 11 p.m., we caught the train back to Finland. As it drew out of the station, I felt a little more relaxed and secure lying in the four-berth sleeper. But I knew that I would not feel really safe until we had crossed the Finnish frontier. One thing was certain: there would be no more jokes about spying on this trip.

It was good to get back to Finland. I enjoyed the way of life there, the teaching and friendships that developed. One of my students was Kalevi Horppu, a young postman: we often went skiing together at weekends. He was Finland's hammer throwing champion and in September '62 would represent his country in an international athletics championship at London's White City stadium. Other friends introduced me to English translations of Finnish literature. I was impressed by the enormous epic poem *Kalevala: The Land of Heroes* (22,795 lines), written by Elias Lönnrot (1802-1884) and based on oral folk legends, poems and stories. It became the basis of Finnish culture and inspired Sibelius to compose some of his most famous music.

Cross-country skiing became my main spare time interest. I spent my next Easter with a mixed party of Finns and foreigners in the north of Finnish Lapland. We stayed in a small village near Enontekiö, surrounded by reindeer herds. One day had fifteen hours of sunshine. The views across the escarpment and moorland were vivid and encouraged us to ski for hours, sometimes competing with reindeer pulling sledges. I amazed myself by skiing nearly a hundred miles during the week, feeling very fit at the end.

In October '62 the Cold War again started to impinge on life. The Cuban missile crisis was looming, with Krushchev and Kennedy preparing for a showdown; and Finnish people, especially those near the frontier with Russia, prepared for the worst. I was told that if wolves were seen coming out of the forests in Karelia it meant that there were Russian troop movements there.

My friend Ulf, who lived near Helsinki, had a yacht based at Pori on the west coast opposite Sweden. He phoned me to say that he was organising emergency food rations and was ready to sail at short notice; if the situation worsened, I was welcome to join him and his family. Fortunately, by the end of November the missile bases in Cuba were being dismantled and the Cuban blockade ended. We all relaxed and tried to look on the bright side of life through the winter gloom.

It was helped by the prospect of Independence Day celebrations on 6th December, commemorating Finland's independence from Russia in 1917, and then preparations for Christmas. Just before it there was the Finnish-British Society's Party, at which the girls' grammar school performed a stage version of Dickens' *A Christmas Carol* in a short adaptation I made. 'The Spirit of Christmas Yet to Come' seemed most appropriate at this time.

3: First Posting

On an April morning in 1965, I was summoned to the British Council's headquarters at 65 Davies Street, London to report to the Director of Personnel. With a feeling of excitement tinged with a little apprehension, I made my way on the underground to Bond Street Station. I knew the meeting was to do with my posting, and my mind started flitting around the eighty or so countries where the Council had offices. Where would I really like to go, or hope not to?

I had joined the Council at the beginning of 1964 and worked for some months in administration in Fellowships Department. Then they had enrolled me for a Postgraduate Certificate in Education at the Institute of Education, London University, with special reference to the teaching of English as a Foreign Language. The course finished in June '65; some time that summer I could expect to be posted overseas, probably to train teachers of English.

It was in a questioning frame of mind that I entered the Personnel Director's office. After a few preliminaries, he said:

"We've decided on your posting: it's to Kathmandu, Nepal. You'll be training graduate teachers of English on in-service courses and working with someone who is already there. I can't give you any details now, but we'll be sending you information and a Record of Living Conditions in due course. You'll be going later in the summer."

As a young man still in his twenties, I could not believe my ears. What an adventure! I walked out of the room almost in shock. What would my fiancée say? I had arranged to meet her for lunch near the Institute of Education. Jane and I had met on the same course and had only been engaged for a couple of weeks. I couldn't wait to tell her about the posting.

"Guess where we're going?"

"I haven't a clue."

"Nepal. You know: Kathmandu... Everest... Gurkhas..." As an afterthought I added: "There's a one-eyed yellow idol to the north of Kathmandu. There's – "

"Yes, but where is it?"

"I'm not sure exactly, but it's in the Himalayas, somewhere near India."

Later, we looked in an atlas and found that, as most people know nowadays, Nepal was sandwiched between India and Tibet. To both of us it seemed distant, remote and exciting, as we had never been out of Europe.

In 1965 Nepal was little-known except for Mount Everest and the overland 'hippy trail', which had started earlier in the decade. Tourism was in its infancy; the country had only been open to the West since 1951, when diplomatic relations with many nations had been established by King Tribhuvan. The Nepalese royal family had been made prisoners in their own palace for more than a century by a dynasty of

Rana prime ministers, who were eventually overthrown in 1951.

Britain's links with Nepal went back to the Anglo-Gurkha War of 1814-1816, in which the British East India Company troops fought the Gurkhas' territorial expansion in North India. It ended with the Treaty of Segauli, or Treaty of Friendship, in 1816, which had established a British Resident in Kathmandu as observer, with no power of interference. From that time on, Gurkha troops had been recruited into the service of the East India Company, as the British had been impressed by their bravery in the war. So began the Gurkha Rifles.

The following month I received information about living conditions and what to take with us. An outline of the work briefly explained my role. I was to train graduate high school teachers of English on five-month in-service courses in Kathmandu, to specialise in the spoken language (especially phonetics), methodology and audio-visual aids. The rest of the syllabus was being taken by Mike Doyle, who was already at post. We would be there for about four years and would be sailing from Marseilles on 17th August.

It was now May. We had final exams to take from 30th June to 2nd July, and our wedding in Mansfield, Nottinghamshire, was arranged for 17th July. We would have a lot of shopping to do for setting up our first home, and there would be a hundred and one things to see to before packing. How were we going to fit it all in?

Late in May I received a climate clothing grant and an outfit grant from the Council. The latter was a help with buying equipment for entertaining official guests. We enjoyed the shopping spree in London and bought a dinner and tea set of Wedgewood china – 'Moss Green' – twelve of everything, together with a set of stainless steel cutlery. (More than thirty-five years later we still have much of it in use.) Fortunately, we were able to rely on a London firm to pack up the household purchases and despatch the crates to Marseilles for our departure.

At the beginning of August, by means of a generous interest-free loan from the Council, I was able to buy a sand-coloured short-wheelbase Land Rover – for £737 and 2 pence. (I could never understand why the tuppence was added.) We had been told that a Land Rover was the best vehicle for driving around the Kathmandu Valley, which had very few metalled roads, most being of compacted earth.

Eventually the 16th of August arrived. Sadness at saying goodbye to our parents at Victoria Station was coupled with apprehension about coping with all the baggage – two trunks and several suitcases – but offset by the exciting prospect ahead. The train journey to the coast, ferry across the Channel and longer train journey in an overnight sleeper to Marseilles were managed without mishap. It gave us time to reflect on all that had happened during the past few weeks. We consoled ourselves with the thought that our three-day honeymoon in York – the only time we could spare – would be compensated for by two weeks on the ship from Marseilles to Bombay. It was bound to be sunny and warm.

After a delay in Marseilles, the passenger-ship *Viet-Nam* belonging to the Compagnie des Messageries Maritimes set sail on 17th August. We were a little startled at first on hearing the name of the ship and hoped it was not an ill omen. Only six months previously the USA had started bombing North Vietnam, and the war was escalating.

Omens were forgotten as we wallowed in the luxury of our first-ever lengthy cruise, travelling first class and in a French ship, with all that it implied for the cuisine. In this respect, we were not disappointed. I had never before had roast guinea-fowl or Danish caviar on toast, nor goose liver paté, nor trout with almonds; and the bottles of red and white wine included with every lunch and dinner were an undreamt-of indulgence. We shared a table for the whole voyage with a friendly Dutch couple who worked in Hong Kong and were returning there after home leave. We also met the Council's Education Officer for South India, who was on his way back to work after leave. He gave us a picture of everyday life in Madras and described what pre-university English courses were like.

After sailing through the Mediterranean and a brief stop at Port Said, the *Viet-Nam* went through the Suez Canal. We stood on deck to see this famous stretch of water, little realising that in just two years' time the Canal would be closed because of Arab-Israeli hostilities. We would be the last Council staff to use this route to Nepal.

As we entered the Red Sea from Suez, the temperature shot up and heat became oppressive. The following day the ship stopped at Aden for a couple of hours, and we were able to disembark to stretch our legs. Our general impression was of houses scattered on the sides of dry, barren, craggy hills and in the port area, soldiers, barracks and endless shops selling duty-free goods. I bought a watch for thirty shillings (£1.50); it proved a bargain as it kept good time for years.

Once in the Indian Ocean, the air became cooler and fresher, which was a relief; the corollary was that the ship started to roll, and seasickness affected many. Sod's law operated in my case: I was sick on the night of the Captain's dinner and Fancy Dress Ball and had to lie down and miss it. Still, Jane enjoyed it and reported all afterwards. The menu sounded inviting: caviar and vodka, lobster, tournedos steak. Never mind. I recovered the next day and was able to enjoy dozing in a deckchair, now and then reading, chatting or playing the occasional game of deck golf or table tennis.

As we approached Karachi, the sea became rough, and the ship rolled from side to side. We had to hold on to our glasses and plates at dinner. Arriving at around 9 p.m. on 28 August, twelve hours behind schedule, we decided to go ashore for a while. Taking the Purser's advice, we hired a horse-drawn carriage for an hour's sightseeing.

Though well after dusk, the streets were still crowded. Of all the shops open, many were barbers – everywhere we saw people having their hair cut. Dozens of people had bedding on the pavement and slept; others had curled up without any bedclothes on the ground or on steps. From the cafés came sounds of music and smells of curry, which helped to disguise the other unpleasant odours constantly with us. We passed a marriage fête, whose celebrations were obviously going to go on far into the night, and trotted through what seemed to be a red-light district, which had brighter lights and gaily painted houses with balconies. The driver, clearly knowing the place well, pointed up and said: "Girls – dancing". For some, this might have been an invitation.

The next morning we went on deck to watch the departure. A crane by the ship's hold loaded crates and baggage from the quayside belonging to newly arrived passengers. Suddenly a crowd of men surged forward along the wharf shouting to the crane driver and waving their arms. Running up the gangway, they stood by the hold still calling and gesticulating. We learned that this was part of an inter-union dispute about who should do and carry what.

Fortunately, an agreement was reached – one man would carry each box. This was managed well enough for the smaller ones, but when a man tried carrying the last and biggest crate alone to the cheers of his mates, he dropped it just as he reached the gangway and barely managed to stop it falling into the water. (It was marked FRAGILE!) The situation was saved by several men rolling it up the gangway onto the ship.

To the joyful shouts and waving of the dockers on the quayside, the ship departed at last for Bombay. Coincidentally the weather worsened, and we spent the afternoon and evening lying on our bunks, trying to ignore the tossings of the ship. This put us several hours behind schedule again, and we did not dock in Bombay until the afternoon of 30th August. It took several hours to get through customs; they insisted on opening our carefully packed and sealed crates of crockery and other household goods. Fortunately, a local Council officer came and arranged for the heavy baggage to go with us by train to Calcutta, thence by road to Kathmandu. He took us to the station; we were just in time to catch the 7 p.m. steam train.

We had an air-conditioned sleeping compartment because we would be on the train for two nights, having to travel well over 1,000 miles. We sat glued to the window for much of the journey, trying to take in the changing landscape, none of which was like anything we had seen before – from urban areas seething with humanity to arid wasteland devoid of people. Near Calcutta the countryside became green, following the monsoon, with lots of palm trees to add to the contrast.

We were intrigued by the system of organising meals on such a long-distance journey. A bearer would bring a menu so we could order lunch or dinner; at the next stop he would telephone ahead so that, when the train arrived at the station, he could collect the trays of food. The second day happened to be my birthday. It was the first and only time I ever celebrated it by eating curry on a train.

We arrived in Calcutta at 11 a.m. on 1st September to be met by heat and humidity, which hit us hard – we had got used to the air-conditioning while on the train for 40 hours. A local Council officer greeted us and took us to a hotel; there we could have a shower and lie down before meeting up with an English couple who had arranged weeks before to take us out to dinner and to do a little sightseeing. We took in impressions of a city overflowing with poor people, thousands of whom were lying and sleeping on the pavements, and roads congested with cycle rickshaws, taxis and overcrowded buses.

I felt that my senses were becoming dulled, bombarded with so many new sensations. There were unheard-of combinations of colour and squalor, smells of food and faeces, sounds of street sellers hawking their numerous wares and services in unknown tongues. Fascinating though it was, the effect of it, combined with the unbearable heat and humidity, was to bring about a state of exhaustion. After 17 days of travelling and excitement, we staggered into the hotel bedroom to lie there looking up at the large rotating ceiling fan. Any feeling of dizziness was soon dispelled by sleep.

Early next morning a Council car took us to Dum Dum Airport near Calcutta. It suddenly dawned on me that this was the place where the soft-nosed or hollow-ended bullets – dum-dum bullets – were first made in the 19th century. To be in India, even for a short time, had the effect of raising awareness of history as well as geography and language.

A small Indian Airlines DC3 took off into cloud, but by the time we were over the foothills north-west of Calcutta most of it had cleared. The flight became smooth, and there were magnificent views as we approached the Kathmandu Valley, which lies at about 4,500 feet above sea level. Roughly oval, it is about sixteen by twenty miles. Between fluffy mounds of cloud, we could see wooded hills and valleys with terraced slopes. On the horizon the snow-clad peaks of the high Himalayas peeped above the clouds.

Then we were over the Valley, descending gradually in ever-decreasing circles, until we had excellent views of the city itself. It was surrounded by green fields of rice, spreading out towards an enclosing ring of hills. We caught the beautiful sight of temple roofs with sun glinting on gold, and I knew that we had certainly found our Shangri-La.

Soon the plane landed at Gauchar Airport. Gauchar means 'cow pasture', and the appropriateness of the name became clear when I saw cattle grazing at the end of the runway. We were greeted warmly by the Council Representative, Lynndon Clough, who us helped through the customs formalities and gave us information about the accommodation he was taking us to. He then looked at me and commented:

"I'm glad you've got a beard. It makes you look older than your 28 years. It'll be useful here because you'll be dealing with teachers and headteachers who will often be in their thirties or forties. They have more respect for an older person. Nepalese men can't or don't grow beards until they're in their fifties, so they'll think you're quite old."

I could not help laughing at this prospect of ageing so quickly in my first posting!

4: Hush Puppies to the rescue

Our early days in Kathmandu were spent adjusting to a totally new way of life in every respect. We were not only setting up home together for the first time but also facing the need to employ domestic staff, better known at the time as servants. This was something expected of foreigners in official positions, and it helped local employment. So we had our first experience of employing a cook, Bishnu, and his brother, Krishna, as a cleaner and trainee waiter, both full-time; Suku, the gardener, and a dhobi, or laundryman, were both part-time.

We lived in a ground-floor flat, rented by the British Council. Mosquito netting on all the windows and a net over the bed had to be got used to; they were certainly needed in September. The weather was quite hot with some rain later in the day. Consequently, nearly every evening three or four pye-dogs took shelter on our doorstep, usually staying there until morning. We eventually grew accustomed to them, also to the chirping of crickets and the sight, every evening, of cows wandering onto a patch of grass that was not fully enclosed at the rear of the house. As a result of their presence, the grass never needed cutting; unfortunately, they also enjoyed eating the heads off the flowers.

A stroll in the hot sun along a local dusty street going towards the city centre encapsulated the whole atmosphere of life there, with its Hindu and Buddhist temples and shrines. The men wore a light-coloured long shirt without a collar; it hung outside their cotton trousers, baggy around the bottom and tight in the leg. Over this they might wear a western-type jacket or waistcoat; they would also wear a small fez-shaped coloured cotton cap – formal ones were black. Women wore suruwal kamij (shalwar kameez), a short dress over loose trousers, if they were young and saris if they were mature or married. People often went barefoot or wore sandals, though wealthier ones wore shoes or plimsolls.

At a street corner people squatted, selling their wares, perhaps vegetables and fruit – potatoes, tomatoes, enormous radishes, ginger and guavas. While walking, we would sometimes be overtaken by local Newari men and women porters, carrying a bamboo pole across their shoulders, with a basket dangling from each end. They delivered produce to shops and wayside stalls.

Cows wandered down the road, meandering into the centre and causing traffic problems. Drivers had to be particularly careful as the cow is a holy animal. The penalty for accidentally killing one could be twelve years in prison, the same as for killing a person.

A little later in September, Mike Doyle, a Colombo Plan expert who had been running the five-month in-service courses since April the previous year, briefed me on the courses and my work. He explained that there were about 200 high schools around the country and the plan was to train one teacher of English from each school. The purpose was to improve their spoken and written English and instruct them in recent teaching methods, then to observe them in practice in schools near the training centre at Tahachal on the outskirts of the city. Mike told me that he and my predecessor had run two such courses, each having thirty teachers. To my surprise he went on to say that we recruited the teachers ourselves with the help of a Ministry of Education official who acted as guide, interpreter and sponsor of those selected.

My interest was immediately aroused. No one had told me in London, nor was it mentioned in the Council report, that I would be involved in the actual recruitment procedure. I had assumed that this was the responsibility of the Ministry and Mike. Nobody had checked to see if I could walk long distances, though I had had a medical before coming. Neither had anyone suggested taking walking boots, nor had I thought to do so. Fortunately, I liked walking but all I had with me was my trusty pair of informal, comfortable suede shoes – 'Hush Puppies'.

The first trip, in mid-October, was short and by jeep, to Trisuli, just out of Kathmandu Valley to the north-west. We stayed a night and visited one school. The second visit, for five days at the end of October, was somewhat different. It involved going to several high schools to the east and north-east of the Valley and travelling partly by jeep and partly walking and trekking up mountains. The weather was appalling, with non-stop rain, cold and mud. On the mountain road we waited in the jeep for an hour before we could get past a landslide.

When we eventually arrived at Panchkhel High School, the only place we could sleep was in sleeping bags on the compacted earth floor in the house of the headmaster, who was away. My diary entry for the following days read:

> **30TH OCTOBER**: Crawled out of sleeping bag on the floor at 6 a.m.. No breakfast available, just a glass of hot, sweet tea. Jeep up mountain to Balephi, then rough track. Found, with difficulty, a porter to carry our bags up the mountainside. Left at 1 p.m. to climb up to Chautara; climbed about 3,000 feet in torrential rain; soaked through with water running down neck. Took four hours climbing and walking to get to Chautara. Found a tea-house: six glasses of piping hot tea in quick succession brought back some feeling. Eventually found the high school, but no key available; broke open a window-shutter and climbed in. What a sight! Bare floors, no desks, benches or blackboards; pupils' individual slates piled up in a corner. Planks of wood lying in heaps on the floor to season before being made into desks. Our only food a packet of biscuits. Got into sleeping bags and had some whisky I'd brought for such cold, wet contingencies. Getting dark. Suddenly a fluttering. There was a bat in the room. The driver hit it with a piece of wood and it dropped into Mike's open briefcase.
>
> **31ST OCTOBER**: Discovered that there were no graduate teachers in the high school and therefore no-one was eligible to come on the course. The headmaster wasn't available. Altogether an abortive trip, wasting two days.

After being back in Kathmandu for nearly a week, Mike and I and Ram Poorna, from the Ministry of Education, were off on another recruitment journey - to the far east of Nepal. This was totally different from the two previous trips. It entailed flying in a Royal Nepal Airlines DC3 to Biratnagar on the edge of the Terai, the cultivated plains bordering northern India; then riding in a British Army Land Rover to

Dharan, the Gurkha Brigade recruiting depot. En route we passed mango trees and fields of rice and maize. We stayed a night in Dharan ready to interview teachers the next day and noticed that in the town people often spoke of the Indian rupee as the 'Companiya rupiya' to distinguish it from the Nepalese rupee. I was amazed to find references to the East India Company, which had ceased to exist in 1873, still in daily use. Truly a link with the past.

There followed nine days of trekking up and down mountains, between 4,000 and 9,000 feet, and along valleys and river beds in order to visit four schools. I found that although it was more of a strain going uphill, with lots of puffing and panting, it was less dangerous than going steeply downhill, with the potential for slipping and sliding on loose stones and rocks. Fortunately, my shoes gripped well and I did not fall.

At one village, Dhankuta, an afternoon was spent interviewing and testing teachers who had assembled there from the surrounding district; two of them had walked for three days to be there. We had to check their sight by asking them to read what was on the blackboard from the back of the classroom and to see if they had any hearing difficulties by speaking to them from a short distance away.

Mike and I had two more days' walking ahead of us, due north, to get to the final school at Terhathum ('13 peaks'), which was at 8,500 feet (2,589 m). A typical day involved getting up soon after 5 a.m., a simple wash if any water was available, a glass of hot tea and, perhaps, a hard-boiled egg. Then on the trail by 7 a.m., stopping for ten minutes in every hour. Distance was not normally measured in miles but in hours: going up a steep track we reckoned on about 1,000 feet an hour. We often passed porters on the track, or they passed us, carrying loads of salt. Sherpas carried heavy loads in baskets on their backs, weighing 60-80 pounds (27-36 kg) supported by a strap over their forehead. The strain on the neck and shoulders must have been enormous.

Between 11 a.m. and noon we stopped for food – usually rice, dhal, potatoes, greens and, if we were lucky and one was available, a chicken. Bed by 9 p.m..

On the last day we were up at 5 a.m. and caught the cold, crisp sunrise, pale blue sky, and the magnificent view of the white Himalayan peaks of Lhotse, Everest, Nuptse and Makalu, about fifty miles away.

The day's walk was sheer joy, crowned by a warm greeting from the headmaster of Terhathum High School on our arrival in the mid-afternoon. Needless to say, we recruited him. We stayed overnight with two Peace Corps Volunteers, who told us about a startling announcement on the radio – Ian Smith had just made a unilateral declaration of Southern Rhodesia's independence (11th November). It seemed incredible to hear this momentous news in such a remote area. At the end of the trek, I calculated that we had covered about 120 miles on foot in the eleven days, and my Hush Puppies were not even squeaking.

5: THE BANK MANAGER

Entering the Nepal Bank, I enquired about opening a foreign exchange account. I was ushered upstairs to the first floor, rising above the mass of humanity milling around, whose hubbub filled the banking hall. An air of mild chaos reigned. The atmosphere was clammy as it was the tail-end of the monsoon, near the end of September.

It felt strange being in a bank on a Sunday morning – Saturday was the weekly holiday in Nepal, with Sunday a normal working day – but this was far from the only unusual experience that morning, as I was to find out.

In front of me a door stood open, the entrance covered by a pale cotton curtain. Above the lintel a notice in both Nepali and English proclaimed, 'General Manager'. I was impressed that for so mundane a procedure as opening an account, I should be seeing so high a personage. The curtain was pulled aside. I entered.

The sight that greeted me was at variance with what I remembered of my one visit to an English bank manager. Around the walls were arranged a dozen upright, wooden-backed chairs; seated on them, chatting loudly, were several men. Their eyes swivelled to appraise me as I came in, but the talking did not cease. Overhead a large fan revolved, churning the warm air sucked in through the mosquito-mesh over the open window and turning it into a welcome draught.

A clerk indicated an empty chair for me to sit on and await my turn. By chance, it was next to the only other westerner in the room, an Englishman who worked as Smallpox Control Officer for the WHO. We chatted to pass the time. Now and then I glanced towards the manager, to whom I had been briefly introduced two weeks previously. He was behind a desk at the end of the room.

When it was my turn, he stood up and gestured me towards the chair at the side of his desk. Putting both his hands together in front of his chest as though praying, he bent his head forward and said in a deep booming voice, "Namaste" ('greetings'). I responded similarly, and we shook hands. He was thickset, in his fifties, with a jovial expression on his plump face. His dress was traditional and smart: he wore a small black hat and a black, western-style jacket over a beige cross-over shirt, with tails hanging out in the national fashion. His beige cotton trousers, which narrowed over the calves like jodhpurs, were smartly pressed. His eyes gleamed behind heavy-rimmed glasses.

We sat down, and I stated my business. It was dealt with fairly quickly and without complications. Meanwhile, the conversations on the chairs behind me continued unabated. Privacy seemed to be an alien concept or, perhaps, simply unnecessary.

The transaction completed, the manager, to my surprise, suddenly pointed down at my shoes and asked: "What are they?"

I could hardly believe my ears: a question about my dust-covered, scuffed, brown suede, mass-produced 'Hush Puppies'.

"Hush Puppies," I said, wondering what this was leading to.

He looked at me uncomprehendingly.

I explained that 'puppies' was the plural of 'puppy'.

"Puppy, I know," he said, "a young dog; but what is 'hush'?"

I explained again.

"So, this shoe is made from a dog?"

"No, they're made of pigskin," I exclaimed and got out of my depth trying to explain why they were so named. I remembered reading how in the USA where the shoes were first made 'Hush Puppies' was a name given to the deep-fried corn dough balls which farmers gave to their barking dogs to quieten them. As 'barking dogs' was also a colloquial expression for feet that hurt, the name 'Hush Puppies' seemed a good name for casual shoes that were easy on the feet.

He held out a hand. It was clear he wanted to examine a shoe. Hesitantly, I unlaced one and gave it to him. He peered inside, felt the suede and looked at the sole; he then handed it back, without saying a word. Clearly he was not impressed. Pointing down at his own shoes, he said: "Church's".

I obviously looked puzzled because he repeated "Church's" and added: "They're Church's, made in England, in Northampton – look".

He reached down, took off his right shoe and passed it to me. No one is going to believe this, I thought – sitting in a bank manager's office comparing shoes!

I looked at *his* offering: it was of black, shiny leather, well-made and expensive-looking. Looking inside, I could see the name stamped.

"I order them, made to measure, from England," he volunteered.

Completely out of my league, I thought. He then proceeded to tell me the cost. Some quick mental arithmetic persuaded me that what he had spent on this one pair of shoes would keep me in Hush Puppies for years. Nor was that the end of it. He casually added that he had a different pair of Church's shoes for each day of the week.

Then he showed me his fountain pen – a Parker, of course. He proceeded to describe his enormous collection of fountain and ball-point pens: British, American, German – so it went on. I felt myself going glassy-eyed and acutely aware of the cheap black biro in my trouser pocket, the only writing implement I ever employed. He asked me what I used. I showed it; he just nodded.

As I put it away, my elbow nearly caught a saucer of water standing on the corner of his desk. I thought perhaps it was to prevent the air becoming too dry, though it seemed rather unlikely as it was very humid. The manager noticed what I was looking at and smiled. Just then a messenger came in and placed a pile of opened and empty envelopes near the saucer.

The manager picked up one and looked at me. "Stamps", he explained and proceeded carefully to tear off the corner with the stamp on it and put it in the saucer of water. Ah, he was a stamp collector. He started to tell me about his collection, all the while prodding at the piece of paper in the saucer with a pair of tweezers that he must have kept permanently on his desk. When the stamp floated and separated from the paper, he picked it up with the tweezers and placed it face downwards to dry on a sheet of nearby white blotting paper. I smiled.

"I collect stamps too," I said. "Mostly British". He returned the smile – a conspiracy between collectors. Briefly I described my areas of specialisation, which included first day covers and Victorian stamps.

His eyes lit up, and he commented: "I also collect British stamps. What is your earliest stamp?"

"A Penny Black", I replied.

He nodded slowly in approval.

From then on, each time I went into the bank, I made a point of taking him stamps. If he spotted me entering the building, his voice would boom across the banking hall, starting deep-down and gradually rising: "Baarb (Bob), I've got something for you", and he would give me some Nepalese stamps. It was stamp-collecting that cemented our bizarre friendship, which continued until I left Nepal four years later.

6: Encounters with animals

In spring 1966, towards the end of my first in-service course, Jane and I were invited by some teachers to join their families one Saturday for a picnic. We set off with my colleague Mike and his wife in their car. It was an ideal day for it, being sunny and very warm.

I had no conception of what a Nepalese picnic was like. Not unnaturally I thought of the usual sandwiches or salad and cooked meats, accompanied by cold drinks or flasks of tea or coffee. On voicing my ignorance to Mike, he said:

"Oh, they always bring the pots and firewood with them and cook the food on the spot. We'll probably have to wait around for a bit while it's going on."

After a half-hour's drive along dusty roads, we arrived at a place near the southern edge of Kathmandu Valley where about twenty-five adults and children had already grouped. Walking and talking along the edge of irrigation ditches bordering rice paddies, we were soon climbing a hill into a clearing surrounded by trees and undergrowth. Following the example of the teachers, we put the rugs we had brought onto the grass and sat down. I noticed it was just after noon and was pleased to see that already someone was building a fire. Peckish, I would be glad when the food was cooked.

I noticed one of the teachers, who had been at the back of the group, was talking to a man leading a goat by a rope round its neck. I had seen him when we had started to walk but had not thought he was with our party. I asked Mike why the goat had been brought along.

"It's probably our lunch," he replied with a wry smile.

Startled, I could not help but watch as the goat was taken to the edge of the clearing. Transfixed by the certainty of what was about to happen, I began to regret coming on the picnic. One man pulled on the end of the rope so that the goat's head was stretched forward, while another held the rear of the animal in a firm grip. Quickly the man who had brought the goat took out his kukri – the Nepalese large and heavy broad-bladed knife, made famous by the Gurkhas. With one downward stroke he beheaded the animal, and the blood spurted from its neck. He wasted no time in starting to cut up the carcass.

I winced and looked away. Having seen enough to cause me to lose my appetite, I started talking with the others to take my mind off it. We all relaxed in the warmth, and the conversation started to flag. After some time Mike said he was starving, and I had to admit that the smells of curried meat and vegetables wafting in our direction seemed delicious. My appetite returning with a vengeance, I was ready for the meal that was finally served up at 4 p.m..

The experience of the picnic made me reflect that in the West we are unused to the sight of blood or seeing animals slaughtered. Some of us, I am sure, would forgo meat if we had to kill the animal ourselves.

Certainly this aspect of life is brought home with a shock in a country such as Nepal, where the killing of animals for food is combined with a religious dimension – that of Hinduism. This may involve sacrificing an animal in a ritual where some of the blood is made as an offering to a god while the meat is eaten by the families.

It was a fairly common sight to see a chicken rapidly despatched with a kukri. The blood would then be smeared on a stone figure in a wayside shrine, a prayer said and the bird taken away for immediate cooking. Animal sacrifice was always functional; no meat was ever wasted. Where most families could only afford one meal with meat in a week, if that, it was highly valued.

Although in time you became conditioned to aspects of life that previously you were squeamish about, there still remained some things that I could not look upon with indifference. Invariably this involved a large animal – the buffalo. The first time I saw a buffalo head being carried in a circular bamboo basket suspended from a pole across the shoulders of a barefoot porter, I was shaken. Many months later, even with accumulated experiences, I still found the sight unnerving, especially when the animal's large dark eyes were staring straight ahead.

Sitting at my desk upstairs, reading near an open window, I was distracted by a commotion coming from outside. It was a bright, sunny day, with a clear blue sky. The noise was at odds with the peaceful view of the front garden and driveway.

Looking out at the lane beyond our closed gate, I noticed that a group of villagers had assembled. From the window I could see only their heads jerking about and their arms brandishing sticks and throwing stones. Then several stones hit and bounced off the aluminium cladding on the large gate. Puzzled, I rushed downstairs to find out what was happening.

Only a few months previously Jane and I had moved to this newly-built house to the north-east of the city centre, just a short walk behind the Royal Palace, in the district of Gairidhara. The house was situated between a paddy-field and a cluster of old houses; our Nepalese landlord lived in a large traditional house in the compound next door. From the upstairs windows we often observed his family in the early morning, washing in cold water from an old pump in the front of their house. The group of houses we called "pig village" because the dirt lanes and tracks around the area were full of small black pigs running around loose like dogs. Our relations with the locals were amicable, so the sudden noise and stone-throwing were disturbing.

I ran down the drive past our parked Land Rover and pulled the gate open to peer into the lane. There was a brown-and-white smooth-haired dog cowering against one of the gateposts and the adjoining wall. When the dog saw the gate open, it darted inside and stood near me, panting. It was indistinguishable from any number of pye-dogs that could be seen any day of the week all around the city.

These stray dogs were always scrounging for food and were nearly always diseased in some way. It was not uncommon to see one waiting behind a child who was crouching by the roadside defecating. When the child moved off, the dog would start its feast. Typically, pye-dogs slept at the roadside or in the shadow of a tree in the hottest part of the day. At night they hunted for rats and mice and added their howling to the deep croaks of bullfrogs and the chirping of cicadas.

I looked at the creature standing near me and backed off a little as some of the men outside shouted at me while edging forward waving their sticks. I could not understand what they were saying, but they were gesturing towards him. I stared at the blood on his back where it had been hit by a stone. He was cringing and quivering and shrank back from the noisy group gathering just outside. I began to feel angry at the ill-treatment of the dog and was about to close the gate in the men's faces when Suku, our part-time gardener, came running up. The men shouted to him and pointed at the shaking creature. Suku called to me: "Sahib – dog – rabies."

Horrified, I paused. There was no time to reflect on the awful dilemma I faced. What could I do? There was no cure for a rabid dog, and I could not risk trying to take him to the one vet in the city to have him put down. If I were bitten, that might be the end of me. The very least that could happen would be a painful course of vaccine injections into the stomach lining once a day for fourteen days. Neither could I chance leaving the dog in the garden while I drove to the British Military Attaché to see if he would come and shoot him. At that time very few private houses had telephones installed.

I felt there was no choice and I had to act quickly. I moved carefully towards the dog, waving an arm to motion him back into the lane. Suku and I grabbed the gate and dragged it shut so that the dog was pushed outside with the men.

Much as I felt sorry for the animal, I sympathised with the villagers, who probably would not stand a chance of surviving if they were bitten. Slow death from rabies was too horrible to comtemplate; they were doing the only thing they could, under the circumstances, with the only weapons at their disposal to keep the dog at a distance – sticks and stones. Feeling sick at heart, I retraced my steps to the house and tried to shut out the yelps and whimpers as the dog went to his certain, painful death.

For two weeks in the spring of 1967 I was based at the Brigade of Gurkhas' recruiting depot at Dharan in Eastern Nepal – not teaching the military, but there for my convenience, arranged by the British Council.

The camp was rather like an oasis. It had well-tended lawns and flowerbeds just like an English country house and exuded an aura of tidiness that was in marked contrast with the hot and dusty roads outside the camp entrance. The depot also had its philanthropic side – it was popular in the area as it provided a regular clinic and first aid post for local people.

One morning I was sitting at a table on the edge of the patio outside the Officers' Mess typing a syllabus for a local intermediate teachers' course. It was hot and sunny, but I was sitting by the lawn in the shade provided by an overhanging wooden roof. Pounding away on my portable Olympia, I was oblivious of everything around me.

Suddenly a British major in the Gurkhas appeared beside me, stooped and quietly said: "Keep on typing. Don't stop, and don't watch me."

I could not help noticing that he was carrying a golf club in his right hand. Puzzled by this dramatic intrusion, I carried on working. As there was so much to get done, I was totally absorbed in the task.

Then I heard a sharp crack close by and swivelled round. The Gurkha officer had just swung his golf club and had clearly hit something. He said: "It's okay now. Come and look."

Totally mystified, I took the necessary few steps towards him and noticed something on the grass. I stared at it in horror. It was the body of a snake. The major explained:

"I just happened to glance out of the doorway when you were typing and noticed the cobra on the lawn. It was coming towards you and had reared up with its hood puffed out. It was probably going to strike soon. I guess it was to do with the typing. Perhaps the clatter of the keys and vibration aroused it. Too risky to try and shoot it, so I got my club."

"What did you do?" I asked, beginning to feel weak.

"Oh, I took a swing at its hood – just like hitting a golf ball – and knocked its head off."

I stared at the headless cobra, which was more than six feet long, and muttered to the major: "Thank you, you've probably saved my life."

He laughed: "Do you want it as a souvenir?"

That was a souvenir I could do without, and to me it was no laughing matter. Another instance of what might have happened. My stars were again lucky.

Snakes And Mad Dogs Killed

Dharan, August 8: Altogether 249 cobras, 13 mad dogs and ten manas of flies have been killed here at the initiative of Dharan town panchayat.

The town panchayat had announced monetary rewards for killing mad dogs, snakes and flies, RSS.

A cutting from *Rising Nepal*... I wonder if the major knew about this!

7: THE END OF THE LINE

As I sat down on the hard wooden slatted seat in the first class compartment, I glanced at the headlines of the paper being read by a middle-aged Indian army lieutenant sitting opposite me.

80% POSTAL RUNNERS HEATSTROKE IN PATNA DISTRICT

The slim, moustached officer saw me peering and shortly passed the paper to me, after complaining about the heat and telling me something of his service in Malaya with Mountbatten.

I read the lead story. All the mail was held up; already fifteen postal runners had died from heat exhaustion. My heart went out to them. I had seen how they travelled on foot, jogging with a bag of mail held over one shoulder and carrying in the other hand a spear to which bells were attached to warn people of their arrival. (The spear itself was for self-protection from attacks by wild animals or dacoits.)

As luck would have it, I had to travel through the extreme north of India in mid-June 1966 – one of the hottest months on record. It was a recruitment trip to interview and select more Nepalese high school English teachers for an in-service course. What was I doing in a train in North India? The answer is straightforward, even if the route was not: it was the only way to get to the two towns in southern Nepal I was visiting, Birgunj and Janakpur. They were in the Terai, the low, fertile, sub-tropical plain shared with northern India. The Terai is often called "the granary of Nepal", as it is the major area for growing rice, maize, mustard, lentils and sugar beet, as well as tobacco. An added feature of some of the jungle areas is the presence of larger forms of wildlife, such as rhinos, tigers, elephants and crocodiles.

Travelling to Birgunj and Janakpur from Kathmandu involved some complicated arrangements. There had been an initial thirty-minute flight in a DC3 from Kathmandu to Simra, followed by a similar length taxi journey to Birgunj. The next stage was a half-hour cycle rickshaw ride over the frontier to Raxaul station, and now came this five-hour train journey within northern India to Durbhanga, with a change of trains and another five hours to Jaynagar. The final stretch was a one-and-a-half hour trip on an old Nepalese narrow-gauge railway back over the frontier to Janakpur. The train on this track had only two carriages. In Nepal there were only about sixty miles of railway lines all told.

I was accompanied on the journey by Mr Upadhyaya from the Secondary Education Section in the Ministry of Education. I got on well with him and liked his refreshingly honest answers and unusual directness. He was a young man, polite, helpful and reliable, who acted as interpreter and organiser of our day-to-day arrangements. However, he was not responsible for the accommodation provided en route; nor could he help the lack of hygiene or amenities. Still less could he do anything about the appalling temperature of 115° F that caused non-stop sweating and a persistent longing to stand under a cold shower.

We had spent the first two nights in the border town of Birgunj at the

Government Rest House. I could not believe the relative luxury. We shared a room with single beds, each equipped with a mosquito frame and net; there was also a table and a chair. The biggest surprise of all was the floor-standing electric fan – an absolute godsend in the heat. The water arrangements were primitive, however. Although there was a sitting-type lavatory and a washbasin and shower-fitting, they were not connected to any water supply. Instead, in the morning and evening a bucket of water was brought up to us. We threw most of it over ourselves and kept some for the toilet.

At the end of the first day, after testing and interviewing some teachers, we walked back to the Rest House along the noisy main street. To the usual hubbub was added the sound of a band playing drums and pipes. A wedding procession was slowly progressing down the road, following the ceremonial elephant complete with its red trappings. That little tableau, together with the dinner of rice and dhal, washed down with water containing a few drops of iodine to purify it, brought home to me just how far I had come since leaving England less than a year before.

During the two days we spent travelling to Janakpur from Raxaul via Durbhanga, along with the friendly Indian army officer, it was necessary to get up soon after 4 a.m. in order to catch the early morning trains and be sure of seats. Janakpur is famous for its Janaki Temple in the town centre, a site of pilgrimage for Hindus from all over the subcontinent. Although there was little time for sightseeing, we did see the temples and walk through the bazaar and stop for a glass of 'chiya' (tea).

The two nights in Janakpur remain engraved on my memory. Someone had forgotten to book us into the Indian Aid Hostel as I had asked; consequently, Upadhyaya and I had to share a small room in the local high school where we were going to interview teachers. It had no beds, just wooden school benches pulled together, on which we placed a blanket. The nets that we tied above the benches did not prevent the mosquitoes finding a way in and biting us sufficiently to ensure that we were constantly disturbed. If there had been a fan in the room, it might have alleviated some of the stifling heat; but even that would not have drowned the screams and singing of the mad woman just outside the window. All in all we managed to get only three hours' sleep.

Everything started to go downhill on the return journey. Two hours' travelling in intense heat on hard seats in the jolting trains were combined with an onset of increasingly frequent attacks of diarrhoea. My dashes along the corridor to the rudimentary toilet were hampered by a need to push through people crowding around the doorway. The situation was not helped by being able to see the track passing immediately below as I crouched over the hole cut in the floor.

In spite of occasional stomach pains, I felt a need to eat something as I had not taken any solid food that morning. But I could not face the thought of curry or anything cooked in a lot of oil. When we arrived at the interchange station at Durbhanga at 3.30 p.m., Upadhyaya and I went to the refreshment room. To my surprise, a menu in English listed tea, toast, and scrambled eggs. Gratefully, I asked the waiter for all of these but was told that the chief cook was not there, so scrambled eggs were not available, only omelette. Knowing how oily it would be, I shook my head.

Upadhyaya explained the problem to the waiter, who suggested we go with him to the kitchen and tell the cook what we wanted. I was pleasantly surprised at this helpful attitude and straightaway followed them to the assistant cook, who looked little more than a boy. For the first time in my life I found myself dictating a recipe – perhaps for disaster!

"Take two eggs and break them into a bowl," I began, miming the actions while Upadhyaya translated. The cook nodded.

"Add a little milk and beat them until they are well mixed." Again he nodded.

"Melt a little butter in the pan and pour in the mixture, stirring constantly." Upadhyaya translated my 'butter' appropriately as 'ghee'.

Once more the cook nodded, then smiled and said "Yes – ome-letta", then started to use a greasy frying pan, the only utensil in sight. At this point I gave up and prepared to eat a little of it, knowing I would regret it later. When it arrived, I *did*... And I *did*.

After a couple of hours in the waiting room, we returned to the platform to climb aboard the 7.10 p.m. train for a final six hours of similar discomfiture as we made our way slowly towards the frontier station of Raxaul, thankfully near the end of the return journey. I made sure that we were sitting near the entrance of the carriage so as to be near the toilet and open window for the breeze. I need not have worried about the window – they were all open as they had no glass. This meant that mosquitoes, moths and other winged creatures from the night constantly flew inside. Between visits to the loo I watched two very large cockroaches crawling around the floor. No sleep was possible and the journey seemed interminable.

At last, at 1 a.m., we reached Raxaul, the end of the line, where we came to a full stop. I prepared to go through the customs and police checks into Nepal; however, the barrier was down and the police said the frontier closed from 10 p.m. to 6 a.m.. We faced the prospect of sitting in the station for five hours and being bitten to death by mosquitoes. If only we could get across the frontier, the Government Rest House was half an hour away and we would have a bed and some sleep.

The attraction of this was too great to ignore. In spite of a stomach in turmoil, I summoned up my reserves of bluff, a ploy that any competent teacher can resort to when necessary, and said to the police officer:

"I have diplomatic status and must be at the Embassy for an important meeting first thing in the morning. This is an international frontier, and it shouldn't be closed. If I am late for the meeting, I shall have to report the reason to the Ambassador. Please open the barrier."

To add weight to my claim, I showed my passport. Inside the back cover I had quickly fastened the top part of an empty packet of Benson & Hedges cigarettes. It was gold and displayed the British royal coat of arms with an inscription. It looked quite impressive and I knew that the policeman was unlikely to be able to read the "By Appointment" logo. I kept this harmless piece of subterfuge for such contingencies. The policeman looked at the gold and the crest and waved us through. Of course I had remembered to cut off the words 'Special Filter Cigarettes' before putting the cardboard into the passport.

We reached the Rest House at 2.15 a.m. and collapsed into the available beds. I was absolutely exhausted by heat, stomach upset and travelling. I just remembered to put my watch forward fifteen minutes – the symbolic difference between Nepalese time and Indian. In spite of all the difficulties, I reflected that we had interviewed and tested thirteen teachers in the two towns and considered that seven of them were suitable for the next course. So, not a wasted journey.

The next morning, a half-hour flight back to Kathmandu brought our journey to an end. It might have been the end of the travelling, but it was not the end of the motions. A few days later I was in the United Mission Hospital with bacillary dysentery. But there were some consolations: it was cool, clean, comfortable and cockroach-free.

Manchester *Evening News*, Monday, June 1, 1998:

Heat kills 800

The heat wave in India has now killed more than 800 people as temperature reached 120° F.

Nothing changes!

8: SEEKING THE SPINY BABBLER

During our years in Kathmandu, Jane and I became enthusiastic about bird-watching. Before going to Nepal we had not been especially interested, having only a cursory acquaintance with a few British common or garden species. Many of the birds are so small, brown and difficult to identify that they are often referred to, even by ornithologists, as 'little brown jobs'.

However, that all changed when we saw the wide variety of birds in the Kathmandu Valley – of different sizes, very colourful and easier to identify. We were not surprised to learn that within the Valley, with the varied terrain of the surrounding wooded foothills of the Himalayas rising to between 7,000 and 8,000 feet, more than 400 species of birds have been recorded.

The earliest detailed observations of Nepalese birdlife were made in the first half of the 19th century by a remarkable man – Brian Houghton Hodgson. He arrived in Kathmandu in 1820 as Assistant Resident and from 1833 to 1843 was Resident, that is, the representative of the politically powerful British East India Company. In the 23 years that Hodgson lived in Kathmandu, there was very little work of a political nature to occupy him. He therefore filled his time with scholarly pursuits, one of which was ornithology. Hodgson's study of Nepalese birds is unrivalled and laid the foundation for later research: he made an incredible collection of 9,512 specimens, representing 672 species. As he, like all the other early Residents, was confined to the Kathmandu Valley, he paid local people to collect the specimens for him. He then had pictures painted of them and made copious notes. In his later years he donated his collection of bird skins to the British Museum.

To return to our own bird-watching, sometimes it was the unusual colouring or shape of the bird that attracted our attention; in other cases it might be its cry. The Hoopoe combined all of these. It was strikingly attractive with its pinkish-fawn body, 'zebra striped' wings and a crest that flared up when it landed or was startled. Its call was a mellow 'poo-poo-poo', given at short intervals.

The largest bird we ever saw was the Bearded Vulture, or Lammergeier. It was brown, with a wing span of up to nine feet. We occasionally saw this bird when we were trekking in the mountains above 10,000 feet. It is more of an eagle than a vulture and not at all like the Black Vultures that were frequently seen eating carcasses on the muddy banks of the River Bagmati on the outskirts of Kathmandu.

At night, two small owls frequented our garden. Their whitish faces glowed in the moonlight as they perched on a bamboo arch awaiting their opportunity to pounce on mice, rats or other creatures. In the daytime, on overhead wires, the Black Drongo, with its long, divided, lyre-shaped tail, would perch waiting to swoop on insects and then return to the wire with its tail bobbing. Equally widespread, as the name indicates, was the Common Myna. In the evenings they would gather in chattering groups. The noise was made up of a variety of sounds which can only be described as mewing, gurgling and chirruping.

Often when I was returning home from work in the late afternoon, I would go along Kanti Path past the Royal Palace. At a cross-roads nearly opposite the Palace was the Kaiser Library and in its grounds, overhanging the boundary wall, there was a large tree whose branches were filled with Cattle Egrets. Their white bodies and yellow bills contrasted with the dark branches and foliage. Like the Myna, they were noisy when in a group. They were also frequently seen near the River

Bagmati perched on the backs of buffaloes or of goats, either pecking off insects or getting ready to pounce on bugs disturbed by the animals' feeding.

Although we armed ourselves with a copy of Salim Ali's *Book of Indian Birds*, the standard work and available locally at the time, and a pair of binoculars, we still needed the guidance of an expert to help us identify some of the species and lead us to their habitats. Who better to do this than the world's authority on Nepalese birds – Dr Bob Fleming, an American ornithologist of distinction, in his early sixties, who had collected more than 700 bird specimens from Nepal for the Chicago Natural History Museum.

Bob and his wife Beth, a physician, had come to Nepal in 1953 and opened a clinic. In 1956 they had started the United Mission Hospital in Kathmandu, Shanta Bhawan ('The Palace of Peace'), with him as administrator and her as chief physician; by the mid-'60s it had 200 beds and was the first modern hospital in Nepal. The Flemings' son, also named Bob, took his doctorate in Zoology at Michigan and followed in his father's footsteps as far as ornithology was concerned. Later, in 1976, the two Bobs produced the first illustrated book of the birds of Nepal.

Bob Fleming Senior loved to share his passion with some of the expatriates working in Kathmandu. He did this by organising birdwatching walks early on certain Saturday mornings. He and his son would each take a small group and walk in the forest and foothills at the edge of the Valley. They would point out distinctive markings and help us to recognise the different species. They also identified bird calls and were good mimics of a number of them.

One particular Saturday, about a dozen people, British and American, met at a spot on the southern edge of the Valley, ten miles from the city, at about 6 a.m.. For all of us this was a special occasion, as we hoped to see a rare species that was to be found only in the foothills of Nepal – the Spiny Babbler, which we knew very little about. We did know, however, that Bob Fleming had seen it in this area a few times. He told us it was very shy and more often heard than seen.

As we walked towards the forest-covered mountain, Phulchowki, we were amazed to see a massive Bearded Vulture gliding near the peak. It was quite unusual to see these birds in the Valley, and we took it as a good omen. Arriving at the edge of the woodland, we divided into two groups, each led by one of the Flemings, and set off walking into the trees where there was fairly thick undergrowth. We walked in silence, now and then pausing to listen to a whispered comment from Bob Senior, Jane and I having been allocated to him. He was a wiry, lively man with a good sense of humour. He smiled as he pointed to a bird all of us knew, the Red-vented Bulbul, which was a little smaller than an English blackbird and just as common, with a reputation for being quarrelsome.

Just then, not far away, we heard a distinctive bird call – 'preep-pip-pip-pip, tee-tar, tee-tar, tee-tar, tee-tar, preep-pip-pip-pip'. Bob put his finger to his lips and crouched behind a clump of ferns, at the same time beckoning to us to keep close. "That's the Spiny Babbler," he whispered. "I'm going to imitate it and see if it will come close enough for us to catch sight of it." He whistled in a similar way.

To our amazement, his call was answered by the original one, now very much closer. We held our breath and crouched even lower as he whistled again. This time the answer came from just beyond the nearby tree. Bob gave one more 'preep-pip-pip-pip' and peered through the ferns. Then there was a rustle on the far side of the tree, and we all stared in disbelief. It was Bob, the son, with his group, creeping around towards us and starting to whistle again.

Father and son gazed at each other for a moment before roaring with laughter. "Just think," said Bob, Senior, "I taught him how to whistle, and now we're two of a kind."

"But not Spiny Babblers!" commented one of the group.

After a chatty reunion, the two groups again split up with promises not to engage in any more whistling. We pushed on quietly and, rounding a large bush, saw a movement in the ferns ahead. We halted next to Bob. Suddenly a greyish-brown bird, looking a bit like an English Song Thrush and about the same size but with a longer tail, darted from the ferns and vanished into some dense undergrowth.

Bob relaxed and said: "That's what you've come to see. That was the Spiny Babbler."

I do not think I was the only one who felt disappointed. Although not expecting to see anything as brightly coloured as Nepal's national bird, the Impeyan Pheasant or Danphe, I had thought it would be less drab. Somehow one expects a unique bird to be extremely unusual in some exotic way. This one was not. It was just another 'little brown job'!

9: ON TOP OF THE WORLD

One of my duties while working with the British Council in Nepal was to attend official receptions. Some of these were cocktail parties at the British Embassy, where we were expected to converse with guests and visitors. Superficially, cocktail parties may seem bright, cheerful, glamorous and sometimes even exciting if there is an interesting VIP present – that is, until you regard attendance as a chore. Standing with a drink clasped in the left hand, the right being kept free to shake hands and grab titbits from passing trays, soon becomes boring.

One of the most irritating aspects is to be speaking to someone, only to see their eyes swivelling around the room as they calculate who to talk to next. The degree of a person's involvement in a dialogue can be measured by stopping suddenly in mid-sentence and seeing if they notice, or telling a most unlikely story and seeing how they react, if at all. After observing party-goers for some years, I learned to divide them into two categories: those who ask questions and thus help to develop a two-way exchange or real dialogue, and those who never ask questions and rely solely on making statements or answering questions. In my experience, the latter are far more numerous than the former.

It was hardly surprising, therefore, that when I received yet another formal invitation to attend a cocktail party at the Embassy at the beginning of August 1968, my heart sank. It was for Saturday evening, and I did not bother to read who the VIP was. I simply reconciled myself to going and turned up, clean and besuited.

Looking around the rather crowded and smoky room, alive with its usual hubbub of small-talk, I noticed a westerner towering head and shoulders above the rest of the guests. He looked about fifty and his face seemed vaguely familiar, but I could not at first place it. I edged closer to him. I am not short, but he made me feel small. I was mainly conscious of his broad shoulders, long craggy jaw, bushy eyebrows and infectious laugh. Standing near me was one of the Embassy staff who took my arm and soon introduced me to the guest-of-honour: Sir Edmund Hillary.

Of course, I knew that he had climbed Everest at the end of May 1953, with Sherpa Tenzing Norgay. At school in London at the time we had all been taken to see the film *The Conquest of Everest*. However, I had only recently discovered that he returned to Nepal regularly each year to repay his debt to the Sherpas for helping him climb the mountain. There was an account of what he and his friends were doing in his book *Schoolhouse in the Clouds* (1964), which I had just read. They were providing primary schools, piped water supplies, hospitals and medical aid; of these what the Sherpas most wanted was schools for their children. The process had started in 1960 when Hillary had asked a village Sherpa: "If there were one thing we could do for your village, what should it be?"

"Knowledge for our children," had been the answer. The people of another village had said much the same thing: "Though our children have eyes but still they are blind!" So started an impressive programme of primary school building in the Solu Khumbu region around Everest. The first school to be built was Kumjung in 1961, followed by Pangboche, Thami and others in '63 and Junbesi in '64.

At the party I found Sir Edmund spontaneously friendly and interested to hear about the teacher-training work I was doing. I explained that, together with a colleague, I helped to organise in-service courses in Kathmandu for high school teachers of English. The teachers were from different parts of Nepal and we had to go to their schools to interview and select them. I added that the visits often necessitated long treks. But I wanted to hear about the primary schools he had established.

"I enjoyed reading *Schoolhouse in the Clouds*," I said, "but once the schools have been built, what goes on inside them?"

He did not reply immediately but, looking thoughtful, changed the subject by asking one or two more questions about Nepalese schools.

He then turned to speak with someone else.

I was excited at having had the opportunity to speak with this man, but from the way he had turned the conversation and then curtailed it, I felt that somehow I had unintentionally irritated him – perhaps by asking a direct question about the primary schools. I left the party feeling disappointed and wondering if I had caused offence.

The next day, Sunday, being a holiday for us but not for Nepalis, Jane and I decided to make the most of a break in the rainy period by going for a short trek into the hills to the north-west of the city. It was only a few minutes' drive to Balaju Water Gardens where we parked our Land Rover. In the Gardens there was a large open water tank full of fish with a row of twenty-two gushing stone spouts carved in the form of *nagas* or mythical crocodile-serpents: the water was considered holy. In a nearby pond was an image of the sleeping Vishnu, God-as-Preserver in Hinduism. Overlooking this were two small temples with several other Hindu deities.

We spent the next four hours walking in the Nagarjun hills, enjoying the trek through the subtropical trees and glimpses of the Valley below. We saw a variety of birds and butterflies but no unusual animals. We had heard that sometimes leopards were seen on the hills and came down to the outskirts of the city at night, hunting for food, sometimes in people's gardens, especially if they kept animals. One morning we had found scratches on the side door of the house and the gardener had said they were made by a leopard. Perhaps it was just as well we did not see one now. We might have been in dire trouble.

The next morning I went into the Council office to collect mail and sort out my programme for the following days. We were between in-service courses, with the next one due to begin on 1st December; October and November would be spent recruiting, and until then I was preparing syllabuses and materials and helping with administrative work. As I passed through the office, Robert, who had succeeded Lynndon as Representative the previous summer, called me into his room and surprised me by a sudden invitation:

"Can you and Jane come to lunch tomorrow – at 1 o'clock? I'm sorry it's such short notice but someone wants to meet you and it's the only time possible." Anticipating my obvious question, he added, smiling: "You'll find out who it is then."

Intrigued by the air of mystery, I accepted. Mulling it over later with Jane, neither of us could guess what it was about.

The next day we bumped along the dirt road in our Land Rover to Robert and Robina's grand house, set in the midst of paddy fields, a little distance outside the city. From the house there were lovely views of the surrounding hills; the distant white peaks were also visible. However, on this day it was not the views that were uppermost in our minds.

On arrival we were immediately taken into the dining-room to meet the other guests. There were only two: Sir Edmund and Lady Hillary. Expecting the usual etiquette of male sitting next to female, I was surprised to find that I was seated next to the great man – this was clearly to be a party with purpose. As soon as we were seated, Ed (as he preferred to be called) wasted no time in coming to the point:

"There are three Sherpa boys from Solu Khumbu who are very bright. They would certainly benefit from secondary education. I'd like to discuss with you a suitable school in Kathmandu. Our organisation, the Sherpa Trust Board, would pay for them."

I mentioned one school in particular that we used for teaching practice on our courses. It was a Buddhist foundation with a boarding facility and stood very close to the Buddhist temple of Swayambhunath to the west of the city. He thought the school sounded ideal as Sherpas were Buddhists and asked if it was possible to see it. I saw no problem and suggested the next day.

Conversation then turned to some of the other projects he was involved in. He had brought medical supplies and volunteers to replace staff at Khunde Hospital, lying at 12,700 feet, which he, together with friends and local Sherpas, had built at the end of 1966. After going to Solu Khumbu, he was going to the Rivers Arun, Dudh Kosi and Sun Khosi in eastern Nepal to try out two jet boats to see if they could be used for transporting goods along the fast-flowing rivers, which were noted for their rapids. He was going with a fellow New Zealander who was a famous driver of such boats and son of the inventor of them. It sounded an exciting enterprise.

After we had returned home, Jane and I agreed that Ed Hillary was a pleasant, frank and unassuming man, seemingly unspoilt by fame.

The next day I met him at the British Council office and took him in the Land Rover to Ananda Kuti High School. We were met by the headmaster and his wife, also a teacher, who had graduated with distinction from one of our training courses. They showed us around and answered many questions. Clearly Ed found everything satisfactory because he then asked: "When can the boys start?"

They explained that the boys would have to be tested first, in November, to see which grade they could enter. If all went well, they could begin at the start of the following term, in mid-February. Everyone seemed happy with the outcome. I agreed to make a date for the test and then arrange with the British Embassy to make the necessary payments on behalf of the Sherpa Trust Board.

I drove Ed back to the Embassy compound where he was staying temporarily. When we arrived, he did not get out of the cab immediately but turned to me and said:

"I was interested in the question you asked me last week at the cocktail party about what goes on inside the schools we're building in Solu Khumbu. It made me think. How would you like to do an inspection tour of the schools? It'll mean observing classes, interviewing teachers, checking inventories, meeting the managing bodies and drawing up a report to discuss. I'll provide a small plane to fly you to Lukla airstrip; Sherpas will meet you with tents and food. I'll draw up an itinerary. It'll last about three weeks and will involve a devil of a lot of walking. Would you like to go?"

I was too excited to say anything but "Yes, thank you". Then I added: "I'll need to clear it first with the Council Rep. I'll let you know very soon." He nodded, giving the impression that it would not be a problem.

Fortunately, I did not have to contain my excitement too long. I dropped in briefly at home before going on to see Robert to get his approval. Jane was as thrilled as I was and said she would like to go too. We agreed that two heads were better than one when it came to observing classes and producing reports.

I went straight to the office and told Robert what had transpired and that Jane and I would both like to undertake it. Robert smiled and said:

"That's fine. You're between training courses at present and the

Council can justify the inspection tour as it is concerned with schools and teachers. Hillary did clear it with me beforehand, but you can go and tell him you'd like to do it and that it's OK with me."

Without more ado I saw Ed briefly and let him know we would both like to go, adding: "When do we start?"

In seventeen days we visited seven schools and inspected four of them, walking a total of 75 hours up and down mountainsides and along valleys at heights varying between 5,500 and 13,500 feet.

We took off from Kathmandu at 6 a.m. on 2nd September. A single-engined six-seater Helio Courier with an American pilot cruised at 100 mph at heights rising to 15,000 feet. Approaching Solu Khumbu in three quarters of an hour, we had an excellent view of Everest but noticed the dense cloud in the valleys. The plane banked sharply, dived, climbed and wove in and out of the valleys for half an hour, trying to find a way in under the layers of cloud to land at Lukla, just over 9,000 feet on the side of a mountain. We had superb views of all the peaks, but our hearts were in our mouths and stomachs churning when, in order to avoid mountainsides, the plane felt as if it was doing 90° turns. Dark rain clouds soon gathered, covering the whole region, and the pilot had no choice but to return to Kathmandu.

Our disappointment was short-lived: we took off again the next morning at six o'clock. Although it was still cloudy, we managed to land at Lukla, flying through mist towards the end of the grass strip and soon coming to a bumpy halt going up the incline. Hillary and his team of Sherpas had built this airstrip in 1964 virtually by hand to make it quicker to reach the Everest region and provide easier access for medical emergencies. The Sherpa Trust Board charity he had set up financed and built the first hospital in the region, at Khunde, completed in December '66. It was staffed by volunteer doctors from New Zealand.

Ed met us at the strip with his jet-boating group, and we were introduced to the two Sherpas who would be with us for the next three weeks. Kanchha was in charge and acted as guide, interpreter and cook, and Kamenru carried the baggage. Kanchha showed his ability by immediately cooking everyone a breakfast of fried potatoes, omelette and coffee. Ed described the itinerary for the trek around the primary schools, focusing on the four to be inspected – Chaunrikharkar, Khumjung, Pangboche and Junbesi. When we reached Khunde, which would be our base for the northern part of the trek, Kanchha would hire two more porters to carry the tents and all the gear for the rest of the travels. Although we would be able to sleep on floors in some buildings, mostly we would be camping. We were not very thrilled at this prospect in view of the approaching heavy rain clouds.

Ed and his party set off to go jet-boating further south while Jane and I took our first steps towards Khunde and the most exciting work-experience of our lives. The start was rather disappointing: rain poured down as we struggled up the valley towards Namche Bazar. We spent the first night in a tent, asleep by 8 p.m. but woken up at 3 a.m. by the sound of heavy rain lashing the canvas. Jane had a slight headache, and I felt a bit weak in the legs: both were symptoms of altitude sickness. Fortunately, they vanished after a day.

Although the weather throughout was mostly cloudy and wet, being the tail-end of the monsoon, we still got the occasional wonderful views of the white peaks of Thamserku, Ama Dablam and the Everest group. Beautiful small flowers of a variety of colours – white, yellow, pink, mauve and blue – grew in profusion in the valleys and on the mountainsides, while eagles soared above. We had our first sighting of yaks and the cross-breeds of yaks and cows – zopkios and zums. They made their presence felt by rubbing against the guy ropes at night.

Hillary was revered throughout Solu Khumbu as though he were king. This was understandable in view of all the projects funded through his Himalayan Trust (as it is now called). In addition to schools, hospitals, health centres and drinking water systems, there were also bridges, forest nurseries and environmental conservation programmes. I admired all that he was doing and was glad to be able to help in a small way. When we told Sherpas that we were visiting schools on Ed's behalf, it was like using a password, opening all doors and ensuring a warm welcome.

We had memorable meetings with many interesting people. We were greeted by the Head Lama at Thyangboche Monastery with the traditional white scarves he had blessed and drank tea with him. We visited the home in Khumjung of Kappa Kalden, an elderly Sherpa artist who had painted many of the marvellous murals in the temples and monasteries we had seen, especially at Thyangboche, and saw him painting a picture for Ed Hillary and ordered two for ourselves. In Khumjung we were escorted around the small gonpa, or temple, by the village elder and shown the famous yeti scalp that had been taken in 1960 to the USA and elsewhere for scientific analysis by Ed and the village elder of the time. The scalp seemed to be made from the skin of a serow, the thick-coated mountain goat-antelope. At Pangboche Monastery we were shown another yeti scalp and skeleton of a hand. Much of our excitement stemmed from the feeling that reality was blending into legend.

One consequence of the wet weather that we had never experienced before was leeches. They managed to get into our hair and clothing by dropping off rocks and trees and climbing up onto our shoes; they then squeezed their way down inside our socks and up our trouser legs. The result was drops of congealed blood on our heads, necks, legs and between our toes. The only way to remove the leeches was to press a lighted cigarette on them so that they released their hold. Every night in our tent we had to carry out a body search and inspect each other's heads. Not an easily forgotten experience!

Near the end of the visit when we were back at Khunde Hospital, the New Zealand doctor and his wife, who was teaching English in Khumjung School, showed us a lovely little black-and-white ball of fluff. It was a Tibetan terrier puppy given to Hillary by a grateful Tibetan at Thami village, which had also been provided with a primary school. Ed could not take the dog with him, so we were offered it. We accepted with pleasure: as it came from Thami and was a bitch we decided to call her Tammy.

At 7.20 a.m. on 20 September, we said goodbye to our Sherpa friends and started loading baggage into the plane at Lukla airstrip. Then we were told that the plane could only take three passengers plus luggage and that there was another man and a couple waiting to return to Kathmandu. The man had priority as he had to catch a plane the next day to Delhi; the husband of the couple had urgent work in Kathmandu, but his wife did not. Jane needed to get back for teaching, but there was no urgency for me, so she got in behind the two men, setting Tammy on her lap and leaving me on the tarmac with the other man's wife, Diana.

In the rush for the plane to get off before the weather closed in, our baggage was loaded without careful thought; consequently, I was left with only what I stood up in, no change of clothing, just a sleeping bag and my duffel bag. "Never mind," called the pilot, "I'll be back for you tomorrow morning at the same time."

I soon understood the meaning of the proverb "Tomorrow never comes". The plane tried to land during the next six days but could not because of low, thick cloud, rain and mist. Fortunately, Kanchha stayed with us to cook, and there was no shortage of food as Diana had a lot of tins and local potatoes were plentiful. We each had our own tent and often had to stay under cover because of heavy rain. At other times, we paced the airstrip, filling holes with stones and soil.

Boredom took on a deeper meaning. To try to keep it at bay, I made a chess set out of a piece of old cardboard and some empty cigarette packets and played chess with Diana for several hours a day. When the doctor and his wife at Khunde heard of our predicament, they kindly sent down more food, some books and candles.

Eventually, early in the morning of 27th September, the pilot managed to land almost blind in a thickening mist. At the top of the slope some Sherpas pushed the plane's tail round to help it on the slippery mud. We loaded our bags and took off within ten minutes before the visibility was reduced even further. Back in Kathmandu by 9 a.m., we were met by a welcoming party – Jane and Diana's husband. Then it was straight back home, a good breakfast and the bliss of lying in the first bath for twenty-six days.

What of the schools we inspected? It was certainly instructive to be in classes and watch the children sitting cross-legged on the floors writing in exercise books on low wooden desks. The teachers did their best with their limited training and resources, and the children tried hard to learn. I wrote a twenty-page report of the inspection tour for Ed. It was gratifying to be informed in the following months that the major recommendations were being implemented. No pun is intended when I say that the trip was the high point of our four years in Nepal.

10: THE NEW BROOM SWEEPS CLEAN

After our four years in Nepal, the British Council sent me to do a course in applied linguistics at Edinburgh University. Jane did the same diploma course and, with the minimum disruption to her studies, gave birth to our first child in the Easter vacation. At the end of April, a letter arrived from the Council in London giving details of my next posting. I stared at it in disbelief and showed it to Jane. Her reaction was similar: "This is just where we didn't want to go."

I was to be English Language Officer (ELO) in Freetown, Sierra Leone, and to fly out at the end of July, when our son Richard would be five months old. We were so disappointed. I disliked very hot, sticky climates and found them difficult. For this reason I had put West Africa as an undesirable area on a Council form. We had been hoping to be sent to India: although this, too, was a hot country, we had so enjoyed our time in Nepal that we were keen to build on our experience of the sub-continent. However, I appreciated that West Africa was quite a large area of the Council's ELT work and was difficult to rule out entirely. As I knew little about the country, I phoned a contact in the BBC: he described it as a "seedy, rundown backwater by African standards". Not an encouraging beginning.

We arrived at Freetown Airport in the afternoon of 31st July 1970. The rainy season was well under way and, as we stepped out of the plane, the heat and rain combined to hit us like a wet blanket. Richard started crying, probably because of the strangeness of the sticky humidity.

We were met by Bruce Smith, the Representative, who was some years older than me. He made us feel welcome and introduced us to Ernest, the Creole driver of the Council's Land Rover. Bruce tried to point out places of interest as we set out on the lengthy drive, but it was virtually impossible to see anything because of the rain lashing the windows and low grey clouds billowing across the sky, obliterating any view of the hills which formed a backcloth to the harbour. My thoughts flashed back many years to when I had read Graham Greene's novel *The Heart of the Matter*, based on his wartime experiences with the Foreign Office in Freetown in the early 1940s. I remembered how the heat and humidity had oozed out of the pages as I read about Scobie and the innumerable mentions of pouring rain, steaming earth, mosquitoes and cockroaches, the clanging of tin roofs and flapping of vultures' wings.

As we negotiated a roundabout in the town centre, Bruce pointed out the famous old Cotton Tree, under whose branches the first freed Negro slaves gathered in 1787 to sing hymns of gratitude for their safe arrival after being transported from England. These 350 or so former slaves were joined in 1792 by another 1,100 from Nova Scotia, marking the beginning of Freetown. A sense of history started to engulf me, especially when I discovered that one of the main roads was named Wilberforce Street after the great opponent of the slave trade in Britain. William Wilberforce had gone to St John's College, Cambridge, in 1776, and together with Thomas Clarkson, who had also gone there, in 1780, and Granville Sharp, he had founded the Society for the Abolition of the Slave Trade in 1787.

The Land Rover began to climb the road leading out of town. It soon reached the top of Tower Hill, overlooking the harbours. Bruce indicated the imposing British Council building of stone and glass, with balconies on three floors, which had been opened in 1963 by the Prime Minister, Sir Milton Margai, replacing the first 1943 office. Bruce said that he would show me around it the next day but now would take us to our accommodation, which was at the top of Hill Station, a further three miles into palm trees and woods.

Hill Station had been built in 1904 for Europeans to get away from the malaria-carrying mosquitoes and tsetse flies common in town. Since the mid-19th century Sierra Leone had been known as the 'White Man's Grave' on account of the large numbers of British who had died at post or soon after. In seventy years, twelve governors and acting governors had died of fevers. In 1872, 25% of the white population had died of malaria, yellow fever and other fevers. Even though this had happened in the previous century, it still made me apprehensive.

As we ascended, the tin-roofed bungalows became more spaced apart. Eventually we reached ours, white-walled and blue-roofed, at 1

Regent Road – the last building before raw jungle took over. Bruce explained that John, who greeted us, was to be our cook and that later, Momoh, the night watchman, would be arriving. A nanny would be arranged to help Jane with our baby, as would a gardener. From our time in Nepal we were familiar with the pattern of domestic help and that it was expected of foreigners to assist with local employment. We were also familiar with the need to check the mosquito mesh on windows, especially the bedroom at night. But we were totally inexperienced at dealing with a sleepless, crying baby, suffering from prickly heat.

The next day the Council LandRover came to collect me; our own car would be delivered in a few weeks. At Tower Hill, I was shown around by Bruce and taken to my office at the top of the building. It was long and narrow, built as a projector room for showing films in the large hall below and still used occasionally for that. He left me there to settle in and then discuss the ELT work with him.

Along one wall there were two language laboratory booths with tape decks and rows of shelves containing used reel-to-reel tapes, about 200 I guessed. I took some down to see what they were; they had no labels on them and therefore had to be played in order to get an idea of the contents. The opposite wall had a large double-doored cupboard standing about seven feet high. I turned the key in the lock, pulled a door open and quickly stepped back as a number of cardboard files and box files fell out. Looking at them and at the dozens of others in the cupboard, I saw that none were labelled or dated or had any indication of what they contained. Turning to the window, I looked down at the flights of steps leading up to the entrance and wondered what I had come to. Several bookcases stretched along a wall under the window, full of what seemed to be new ELT books – grammars, practice books, course books, readers. It was not obvious why they were all there. Certainly I had something to discuss with Bruce.

In his office I described what I had seen. He nodded sympathetically and explained that he had taken over the post about a year before; the previous holder had been ill and consequently repatriated. My predecessor had been at post for four years instead of the usual two and tried to be transferred several times, but there had been delays. He had become ill and could not do all his work. As for the ELT books in the office, they were for Council presentations to schools and colleges; when I had time, I could decide where to distribute them. Regarding the ELT work, there was no specific job: I would need to discuss matters with the Ministry of Education and offer my services.

That evening I explained all this to Jane. I felt more depressed as I did. For the first time in my life, I actually cried myself to sleep because of a job situation. A little later Richard started crying in his cot and woke us. What a depressing night we had!

The next few weeks were spent in exploring ELT work prospects. This involved discussions at the Ministry, visiting Milton Margai Teachers' Training College for primary school teachers, visiting several secondary schools in the Freetown area and having discussions with the staff at the Institute of Education, University of Sierra Leone at Fourah Bay. I then considered the chaos in my office, decided on a course of action and put my proposals to Bruce. He wasted no time in agreeing with them.

On my visits to schools I had noted that head teachers invariably kept bookcases locked, as they were responsible for anything missing at the annual inventory checks. Many of the books were old, mostly pre-1950. My idea was to offer the Council's book donations partly on a one-for-one basis: to exchange one old one for a new one, and allow teachers to use the books. I also proposed setting up class libraries of supplementary readers.

The training colleges had no syllabus for English for their trainee primary teachers, just an exam at the end of their course set by the ELO in conjunction with the Institute of Education. I proposed visiting some colleges each month, discussing the matter with staff and arranging a seminar at which we could devise a syllabus with appropriate books. In addition, some of the staff could help with the annual Council in-service summer school for teachers.

A new director of Radio Sierra Leone had recently been appointed, a New Zealander named Graham. We talked over ways to promote ELT in programmes for schools and the advice that I could give. This had long-term possibilities.

Sitting in my office, I pondered the various options that were emerging. All were possible, but the main thrust should be with the training colleges and helping them with the syllabus, exams and in-service courses. I decided to give the two language lab booths and all the tapes in my office to Milton Margai College to add to the few they already had: at least they would be used there. With a final glance round the room, I set my thoughts aside, jumped to my feet and went to explain my plan to Bruce. He nodded and I called the driver.

Ernest looked surprised when I told him what we were going to do but helped me to carry all the unlabelled files from the cupboard down to the yard at the back of the building. Soon we had built a bonfire, and he brought out a couple of other local staff to see it before putting a match to it. Clearly it was a new experience for everyone; I hoped it would be the last of its kind. Rather than waste weeks ploughing through the files to see what they were about and if they might be of use, I decided to start virtually from scratch. The flames lighting up the yard lifted my spirits.

All was not gloom, though changing shirts twice a day because of the humidity became tedious. Visiting the training colleges proved interesting and worthwhile, and there was enthusiastic co-operation in devising a syllabus. An unexpected dimension when driving to the colleges was the sight of pythons by the roadside, sometimes writhing in front of the Land Rover. After the rainy season passed, from November onwards, we were able to take Richard to the sandy beaches.

Seeing palm trees at the edge of the shore was a new experience; so too was watching pineapples grow in our back garden. Everyday sights included black monkeys with white flashes swinging through the trees on one side of the garden. Snakes and scorpions were fortunately not so common but enough of a hazard for us to keep Richard close at all times. On one occasion we saw a seemingly endless column of army ants wend its way through the grass and go down the drain under the house and out the other side with a scorpion on the ants' backs.

At the end of the rainy season, I was standing in the garden late one Saturday morning when the chattering of the monkeys in the trees nearby died away. Their noise was replaced by that of laughter and loud voices. Soon I could see smoke rising and hear the sound of wood crackling as it burnt; before long it was followed by the distinctive smell of roasting meat. This was coming from the direction of our nearest neighbour, the Minister of Agriculture, who lived about twenty yards down the hillside in a large bungalow with a rusting iron roof. His property was surrounded by palms and the large spiky green leaves of pineapple plants.

John explained that the barbecue was intended as a thank-you for the Minister's political supporters, henchmen and bodyguards. Each Saturday followed the same pattern, but it never ceased to fascinate me. I always waited for that moment when the first vulture would alight on the apex of the corrugated iron roof with an ungainly flapping of wings. In quick succession others would join it, until there were between twelve and twenty spread along the roof. With heads jerking up and down, they would peer at the roasting meat, looking like clockwork models.

The vultures would have to wait till the party was over, but then their turn would come. They would compete with the guard dogs for bones and scraps, sometimes flapping up to the roof to enjoy a juicy morsel virtually snatched from the jaws of the latter. The vultures looked like sentinels, guarding the bright blue skies around the bungalow of the Minister of Agriculture. As things turned out, there would be good reason to be on one's guard.

11: NOTHING BUT MUSIC

I went to work as usual on Tuesday 23rd March 1971, arriving at the office at 7.45 a.m.. We started early in order to avoid working in the midday heat. Bruce was away, and I was nominally in charge. That only seemed to have any meaning when I was called upon to sign pieces of paper authorising varying degrees of expenditure. This morning was no exception. Mary, the administrative officer, a local Creole who had been with the Council most of her working life, was very efficient and by 8.30 had all the paperwork ready for me. I added my signature to a few chits and stood up to take the papers back to her. It was then that I heard the first shot.

It was followed in quick succession by several more that seemed to come from somewhere near the bottom of Tower Hill. I thought it was the army in Wilberforce Barracks, though I had not heard them shooting like that before and it seemed too close. Perhaps they were on manoeuvres. I looked through the window, but all I could see were some soldiers in khaki uniform carrying rifles and moving around in a street far below. It was not obvious what was happening.

"Mary," I called out. "Come here please".

She ran into the room, looking rather nervous.

"Have you heard the shooting? What's going on, do you know?"

She was shaking her head when Ernest came in, having arrived with more mail from the town centre. Just then we heard the sound of machine-gun fire closer than the rifle shots. Ernest peered out of the window and dropped to the floor. Mary and I followed his example, keeping away from the expanse of glass.

Ernest then spoke: "Army fighting, sir. Try to kill Prime Minister. He is not there. Now army fighting itself."

It seemed there had been an attempted coup against the Prime Minister, Dr Siaka Stevens. Now different factions in the army were fighting each other. From the sound of the shooting, the fighting was spreading around Tower Hill.

I shouted out to the other staff to keep away from the windows and told Ernest to go down and lock the front and back doors. I asked Mary to turn on Radio Sierra Leone to see if there was any news. She did so, but there was nothing but music, some of it ominously martial.

I sat there wondering what to do. The first thing that came to mind was Jane. She taught part-time in a girls' grammar school down in the town, but today she would be at home with Richard, who was now one year old. I was concerned that she was so isolated but reflected that that very fact might be an advantage. Apart from the Agriculture Minister, the nearest person was a brigadier in the army, John Bangura, whom we had never met. He lived about 200 yards down the road.

I phoned Jane and explained briefly what seemed to be happening, warning her not to go out and keep the gates and doors locked. Not that she was likely to go out, as she had no transport – I always used our white Austin 1300 to get to the office; no buses went up to Hill Station.

"I've just this minute been listening to the BBC World Service," she said. "It mentioned an attempted coup in Freetown, with a part of the army rising up against the Prime Minister. It said that a disaffected faction in the army is fighting and trying to persuade others to join in. It ended by saying the situation was very fluid".

I reported this to Mary and Ernest and asked Ernest to keep a careful watch over the approaches to the Council building. Mary kept the radio on for any news while I tried in vain to focus on work. I reflected that the World Service was invaluable in times of crisis, as it was often the only source of news; then my thoughts were interrupted by more rifle fire, which seemed to be just below our building. It was followed by some loud banging on the doors at the front. I called out to Ernest to see what was happening. The banging suddenly stopped as I heard Ernest open the doors, then bolt them again. He ran up to my room and said:

"Sir, two soldiers want to see you."

They were just behind him, carrying old .303 rifles, reminders of my National Service. I began to sweat more than ever.

"Stay here with me, Ernest," I asked as the two young soldiers walked in. Both made a kind of bow and held out their rifles to me. At the same time they said something to Ernest in Krio. Ernest explained:

"They want to surrender, sir".

I stared at them, feeling out of my depth. "But we're not the army."

Ernest continued: "They leave guns and uniform and go out back."

Before I could say more, the men had put the rifles on the floor, started stripping down to their singlets and blue shorts and were escorted to the rear door by Ernest. When he returned, he commented:

"Now they in street and no-one knows they are army."

I handled the rifles carefully, noting they were loaded and that the safety catches were on.

"Mary," I called out. "Please phone Wilberforce Barracks and ask for an officer to come and collect the two rifles."

Very soon a captain and two privates arrived in a jeep to collect the weapons. They seemed amused that the rifles had been surrendered to me but were clearly pleased to have them back. I failed to see the humour in the incident and was only thankful that the rifles had not been fired at us.

Shortly after, we received a phone call from the British High Commission to say that we should leave the office, get home when it was safe to do so and stay there until we heard on the radio that things had returned to normal.

The next morning the music on the radio was interrupted by an announcement from the Force Commander, Brigadier John Bangura. He stated that the army was taking control of the situation. I could not help wondering which situation he was referring to. Matters were not helped by a second announcement a few hours later by another army officer who said that a large proportion of the army dissociated itself from Bangura's declaration. I tried to imagine what it was like in the Radio Sierra Leone building: the director no doubt under lock and key, while the staff were bullied by the army into playing nothing but music. During that day the microphone was grabbed by various factions.

'Normality', as it was called, returned a day later, though people talked of nothing but the attempted coup. The government-controlled radio played down the events, simply reporting that the ringleaders in the breakaway army faction were being hunted. Five days later, Brigadier Bangura and five other officers were arrested in connection with the uprising; the same day, a defence pact was signed with neighbouring Guinea, and their troops entered Sierra Leone to help keep order.

Quickly the political situation deteriorated. On 1st April the Governor-General was sacked, and on 19th April Sierra Leone declared itself a republic, albeit unconstitutionally. It had been independent since 1961 and had stayed within the Commonwealth. However, this was not the first time that the army had revolted. It had overthrown the government in 1967, but constitutional rule had been restored in '68 and Siaka Stevens had become premier. Now, in mid-June 1971, the army officers supposedly involved in the attempted coup were court-martialled and, on 25th June, they were sentenced to be executed. No appeal was possible under a new law. The hanging took place on 29th June.

The local English language newspaper *Unity* carried a banner headline on 1st July:

BANGURA WEPT LIKE A BABY

Former Force Commander, Brigadier John Bangura, who was executed this week, went to the gallows weeping like a baby... Brigadier Bangura had to be bodily carried out of his cell by six men. He resisted stoutly and was said to have been screaming so much that other prisoners were aroused from sleep. Almost up to the end, the Brigadier was reported to be begging for mercy, and crying all the time. His last wish was for the sacrament to be administered to him, but it was too late.

This was the officer who lived a short distance from us. Many thought he was being made the scapegoat for others' offences.

The political situation became increasingly uncertain and cast its shadow over our daily lives. It made it difficult to work with some educational administrators, as they were unsure about future arrangements. In addition, some of them took the opportunity to leave the country. This, combined with the continuous discomfort caused by the terribly hot and sticky weather, made us look forward to our departure on 31st July. Although we were relieved to go, we were sorry to be leaving colleagues and the good friends we had made at the university, training colleges and schools.

We set sail for England on the Elder Dempster Lines m.v. *Aureol*, going by ship so that all the heavy baggage could accompany us, and arriving at Liverpool on 9th August. I thought how apposite that our journey should be the reverse of that used by the freed slaves and to the same port where many of them had originally been brought.

12: THE CENTRE OF ATTENTION

Near the end of September 1978, we spent twelve lovely days in the Azores, taking part in a teacher-training course on Terceira, one of the nine volcanic islands in mid-Atlantic, about 800 miles from Lisbon. Four instructors – Alan, who lived in Lisbon, Rob, Roger and myself – stayed in Angra do Heroismo, the regional capital and enjoyed the unusual volcanic beauty of the island. One memorable sight was the wonderful blue and pink hydrangeas that grew wild everywhere – by roadsides, in fields and at the foot of the mountains. Another was the grapevines trained up against low lava walls in order to avoid the strong winds.

The feeling of contentment that surged as the course approached its end was suddenly destroyed by an announcement on the local radio that the pilots of SATA, the airline of the Azores, were going on strike, supported by TAP, the Portuguese Airline. This could have only one consequence for us: we would be stranded on the Azores until the strike was over. It would cause excessive delays and problems for Roger and myself, as we had to return to our work in the UK. So on the last but one day we tried to think of ways of getting ourselves off the island.

Fortunately, and to our amazement, the local Ministry of Education intervened and arranged for us to be airlifted to Lisbon by a Portuguese Air Force Hercules. The three-hour flight was an interesting experience, sitting sideways along the fuselage, with no windows to look out of: they were small and high up and out of reach, as the plane was normally used for army freight or paratroops. We could not help wondering what it felt like to bale out.

In a state of subdued excitement we landed. It was Friday evening, and we agreed that we would meet at Alan's flat the next afternoon and go early for a farewell dinner before dispersing to our various destinations. Alan said that he would take us to an area where we should be able to find a good and inexpensive restaurant.

Late on Saturday afternoon we met him and two other teachers, Carol and Sue, and walked through the narrow, winding streets of Lisbon's oldest residential area, the Moorish quarter of Alfama. As we strolled in a labyrinth of crooked stairways and alleys, we agreed that Alfama was the most fascinating part of the city and could only really be appreciated on foot. The sun's rays bounced off the red and orange rooftops and beamed down on the yellow-ochre walls, which in their turn reflected them onto the mosaics of pavement, adding to the patterns of colour. Elsewhere, by contrast, there were deep shadows.

After struggling up some steep, twisting streets with a delicious smell of grilled fish at every turn, we followed Alan up five steps into a passageway leading to Beco do Azinhal – the Alley of Oaks, though none grew there. The passage opened into a small cobbled courtyard, enclosed on all sides by four- and five- storey buildings, covered with the usual flaking yellow and orange pastel paint. Apparently it was one of the oldest parts of Alfama, pre-dating the 1755 earthquake that had devastated Lisbon. There were a dozen doorways around the courtyard, each with a peeling white frame, which constrasted with their faded dark green double doors. Alan walked towards numbers 7 and 7A, which formed Restaurante Lautasco.

Dominating the centre of the yard was a tall poplar tree. Its base was surrounded by cobbles and its lower branches trained along outstretched wires to form a canopy above the few wooden tables grouped between it and the restaurant. Every part of the courtyard was overlooked by windows at different levels, many of them fronted by wrought-iron balconies. Washing was flung over several of these; laden clothes-lines were stretched between others. Looking up at the sky, I had an impression of being in a large drying room.

Alan returned with a waiter, who quickly put two tables together so that the six of us could have dinner in the open under the branches of the poplar and enjoy the late September sunshine and warmth. Traditional starters were soon brought – crusty bread rolls and butter with olives – and a bottle of the red house wine. I studied the menu, helpfully translated by Alan, and took the advice of Sue to try the espadarte – grilled swordfish steak with boiled potatoes and a large mixed salad.

Sipping the wine and nibbling the fresh bread, I relaxed and took in the surroundings. I found it strange that we should be eating in such a setting. On many of the balconies, old women dressed in long black skirts or dresses were standing talking, often calling across to their neighbours. I felt that we were on the stage of a theatre-in-the-round, surrounded by an audience in the galleries, waiting for the performance to begin. It was going to be an open-air dinner with a difference, I sensed. This was confirmed by the opening scene.

No sooner had we started to eat than a man in a singlet roared into the courtyard on a small motorbike, swerved round our table and drove straight towards the double doors in the corner, just beyond the restaurant. He bounced up the two steps in front of the doors, edged them open with his front wheel and drove inside. The noise of the bike's reverberations around the small yard startled us and made us wonder what we had come to.

"What on earth's going to happen next?" asked Rob, voicing all our thoughts.

After eating and chatting for a few more minutes, the question was answered. A fat man walked towards us, veering to one side and wobbling as he did. He was in his forties, wearing baggy beach shorts and carrying a large coloured beach ball under each arm. He aimed towards another of the green doors, kicking it open and pushing his way in. I forget who said: "Hasn't he got big balls!"

Clearly we had chosen the right place for ready-made entertainment, though I was not yet sure if pantomime was the best description.

Things seemed to quieten down and our own talk became more animated, especially as we were now on to another bottle, this time the deep red and fully fruity Dão, my introduction to what was to become a favourite wine. We were laughing at the characters we had so recently seen when a couple of elderly women in black entered the courtyard, chatting away and seemingly oblivious of our presence. They walked across to the far side and stopped under one of the balconies.

Several women, also elderly and in black, began calling down to them and pointing in our direction. Questions and answers seemed to be thrown up, down and sideways, with the occasional arm flung out pointing towards us. Just as we found the comings and goings in the courtyard intriguing, so it seemed the inhabitants found us. Was it because we were foreigners and dressed differently? Well, certainly we weren't wearing beach shorts. Was it because our voices and laughter were becoming louder (though we were certainly not drunk)? Or had they understood some of our comments about the washing? As I looked around I noticed one little old woman peeping down at us from behind some laundry. Perhaps she and the rest were waiting for the scene to change.

They did not have long to wait. Four children rushed into the courtyard holding balloons and ran in a circle around our table and the

145

tree. Three of them seemed to be chasing the fourth, but that did not stop them chattering and peering at us. Suddenly they ran into one of the doorways. No sooner had that happened than the adjacent door flew open and a family with two children emerged. The scene had all the appearance of a Whitehall farce – slapstick comedy with somebody rushing in one doorway and somebody different appearing out of another one.

As we finished our meal with black coffee, the voices from the balconies seemed to get louder. We realised that the constant stream of traffic to and fro must be normal and simply an expression of life going on, despite the restaurant's customers. We might have seemed like trespassers in their backyard. Probably the regulars ate much later than we did, after the through traffic had quietened down; so they found it odd and interesting to see us eating early. After a final look round, we left the site of what became known as 'the dinner with never a dull moment'. From the point of view of the spectators, it might have seemed like *dramatis personae: exeunt*!

13: WORK WITH A DIFFERENCE

At about 11 a.m. on Thursday 9th September 1976 I received a phone call that was to change an ordinary morning into an extraordinary one. I was at Manchester University directing a four-week intensive pre-sessional English course for a group of fifteen budding teachers of English from China. They were British Council exchange scholars in their mid-twenties – the first group of teachers we had ever had from the People's Republic.

The call was from the Chinese Embassy in London. After receiving the message, I went straight to the class, which was practising in the language laboratory. I whispered to their tutor, who stared at me in shock, then nodded.

Speaking into his headset microphone, I addressed the teachers: "Please take off your headphones and listen to me. I have an important announcement." Taking off my headphones at the same time, I continued: "I have just received an urgent phone call from your Embassy in London. They have asked me to give you the following news. I regret to have to tell you that Chairman Mao has just died. I am very sorry."

Mao was 82 and his death not entirely unexpected, but the effect on the group was dramatic. Three of the men immediately burst into tears, while all the others looked stunned. No one spoke. I whispered again to the tutor; he announced that the lesson would stop for the time being.

The teachers' leader came up to me; I took him aside and told him that he could use our phone to contact his Embassy. Solemn-faced, he did so and reported back. I suggested that the class might like to take the rest of the day and the Friday off, until they had time to get over their shock. Clearly they were all taking the news personally.

"Thank you," he said, "but we will continue to work. Chairman Mao would want that." I did, however, insist that they stop until after lunch. There was another week to go before the course finished.

The death of Mao Tse-tung brought about the end of the Cultural Revolution, which had started in 1966. During that time the Red Guard, formed mostly of young people, with units in schools and colleges, had set out to destroy any signs of bourgeois culture and bureaucracy. For the first few years, many universities were closed; this had a knock-on effect throughout the education system.

Three years later, I was to learn something of the impact of the Revolution when I received an invitation from the British Council to go to China with two others on a two-month course for teachers of English. The course was at the University of Nanjing on the River Yangtze.

Leaving London on 28th February 1979, we had six days of travel via Hong Kong, Canton (or Guangzhou) and Shanghai before reaching Nanjing, or Nanking as we knew it. Comrade Wu, Lecturer in English at the University, was assigned to us as guide, interpreter and mentor throughout our stay. Charming and friendly, with a good sense of humour, Wu introduced us to the forty-one other teachers on the course, and we were under way.

The first days were a real eye-opener as we discussed with the teachers their experience and needs. It was then that I heard about some of the happenings during the Cultural Revolution, which had affected nearly all of them. One woman described how she had been taken from a class by the Red Guard and transported to Inner Mongolia without being able to contact her family; there she was placed with herdsmen and had to herd yaks for two years before being able to return home. Many teachers were made to do manual work for years, especially in farming communes, tilling fields and growing rice and wheat, and separated from their families.

One teacher asked me if he could possibly have any British stamps that I might receive on mail from England. He loved collecting stamps, but philately had been abolished during the Revolution, as it was considered to be a bourgeois hobby. All of his stamp albums, kept since childhood, had been burned. Now he wanted to start again.

Wu and the teachers explained that when the Revolution had finished, there came an air of liberalisation and everyone wanted to learn a foreign language so as to make contact with the outside world. This explained what became known as 'the English fever' and why I saw groups of students at the University standing on dark evenings under a loud speaker attached to a lamp-post listening to 'English by Radio' relayed from the BBC. Even when it was cold, windy and wet, they tried to write down what they heard and repeat it.

Wu also told us that we were the first British people to visit Nanjing since the early '60s and that everyone would want to look at us. This explained why when we were first taken to the main shopping street about a hundred cyclists collided into each other as they stared, especially at me, being tall and bearded. On entering a shop, we were surrounded by people curious to see what we would buy and how we would pay for it. There was no aggression in this behaviour, just friendly curiosity. I came to know what it must feel like to be an animal in a zoo!

During the two months in Nanjing, I observed that education was taken very seriously, with everyone highly motivated and working very hard, not only in the classroom but also in games and sport. I discovered this personally when being shown round a primary school. The children were playing table tennis; I watched with interest and was invited to join in. A seven-year-old boy beat me easily, three games in a row. I was impressed by everyone's capacity for self-restraint and for enduring hardship. People were usually shy in front of strangers but ready to laugh when the ice was broken. They aptly described themselves as 'like thermos flasks' – cold outside but warm in.

At the beginning of our third week, Wu informed us that there was to be an official university banquet in our honour. Did we know how to use chopsticks? We said we had tried using them in Chinese restaurants in Britain, with varying degrees of success.

"I will give you your driving test in using shopsticks", Wu said. "See if you can pick up a peanut!"

After several efforts, and some tuition, all of us passed. The idea was to think of the chopsticks as being like one's upper and lower jaws; just as only the lower jaw moves, it is only the upper chopstick, held between the thumb and forefinger, that moves to secure the food between the sticks. With some misgivings, we felt ready to tackle the banquet, to be held in the Overseas Students' Canteen. We had already met a few British and American students at the University who were studying Chinese language and literature.

A large circular table was formally and beautifully laid with a starched white table cloth and colourful settings. At each place was a large dark pink plate with a white and green floral design and two polished dark wooden chopsticks. Above the plate was a small blue and white bowl for rice, with a matching china spoon for use with soup courses. All of this was in stark contrast to the bare grey walls and stone floor of the hall, illuminated by strip lighting. There was no heating; it was very cold; small wonder that we kept our overcoats on over our suits or Chinese blue uniforms which our hosts wore.

I looked around at my fellow diners. Apart from the three of us from the Council and Wu, there were ten officials, including Professor Fan, the Vice-President of the University, and Professor Liang, Professor of English, along with Comrade Lin, who was Party Secretary for the English section of the department. Professor Liang, who was 76, had been at university in the USA in the 1930s and then in the UK in 1939; Professor Fan had been at Balliol College, Oxford, in 1945-46, and was now 75. He was very conversant with English literature and had an excellent memory for names and places.

I asked Lin, on my left, how many courses there were in a formal banquet such as this. He said it varied, but it was usually an odd and large number: 11 up to 23 would all be quite normal. He told me of a French diplomat who had sat at the same table many years before: he had misjudged the number of courses and had overeaten and drunk too much. As a result he had collapsed and had to be carried to his room. This was a warning. He sensibly cautioned me to pace my eating. However, this did not prevent him from frequently helping me to more of the tasty items from the central dishes.

In the event, the banquet consisted of thirteen delicious courses, including carp, shrimps, prawns, chicken, Nanjing duck, soups and a variety of vegetables. It seemed that after almost every course, one of the Chinese hosts proposed a toast with the rice spirit or wine and made a little speech. Some were in Chinese, and Wu translated for us. Some were personal, and each of the three of us received one in turn. When it came to my turn, as the youngest of the three guests, Professor Liang proposed "To youth!". I could only respond by proposing "To eternal youth!".

Eating the never-ending courses with chopsticks proved to be not so difficult. The plain boiled rice was easiest to manage: it was put into the small bowl which you lifted up close to your mouth and simply scooped the rice in with the chopsticks. The main problem was trying to cope with so much food. When I realised that we were to keep and use our large plates for every course, except the soup, I was puzzled at first with what to do with all the fish and duck bones that were piling up. I looked at the plates of my Chinese neighbours and could not understand how they could be devoid of bones. Surely they were not eating them all? Then I noticed someone dropping something onto the floor just at the side of his chair. I looked behind me and noticed little piles of bones near the man sitting on my right. That explained the crunching noises I had heard as the waiters brought us more dishes. The contrast between the beautiful white table cloth and the mess on the floor could not have been more marked. It went against the grain for me to drop the bones, so they stayed where they were.

The banquet came to an end with the last item being placed on the table. It looked like a large round pie, sitting in the middle of a silver platter. I could see that Wu was mystified by it. Before it was served up, there was a short speech from Professor Fan. He explained, in English, how he had enjoyed some of the food he had eaten at Oxford. One thing had stayed in his memory for more than thirty years – lemon meringue pie. He hoped it would be a lovely surprise for us. After careful research, he had found a recipe and asked the kitchen staff if they could make one in honour of our visit.

We were impressed and flattered by this gesture. The feeling was, however, tinged with concern about eating the pie. A fairly large portion was put on my plate, to one side of the accumulated debris. With no knife to cut it into manageable pieces nor spoon to eat with, I endeavoured to break it up with one of the chopsticks. I could only break some of the pastry with short stabbing motions; the filling clung to the sticks and created a sticky mess. The more I squeezed the chopsticks to hold a piece in place, the more the filling oozed out and started dripping off. I noticed that I was not the only one having difficulty, but no one else had a beard that insisted on having a portion!

The English course finished at the end of April. After that we were treated to a week's holiday in Beijing before flying back to London. The whole visit was deeply involving, and the many fascinating and moving stories the teachers told us – even some about the usefulness of matchmakers! – added a new dimension to my overseas experience.

14: WE SHALL OVERCOME

In early December 1982, I flew to Greece at the invitation of the British Council. I was to spend two weeks giving talks and running workshops and seminars for teachers and university students on aspects of study skills, especially listening activities. Starting with four days in the second largest port in the country, Thessaloniki, I would then fly via Athens to Ioannina for a night and then back to Athens for a second week's activities. I was looking forward to the trip, as I hardly knew Greece; I had only been to Athens once, for a few days' holiday in 1967 at the time of the military junta.

Everything went well in Thessaloniki – Salonica as I had always known it. I enjoyed the sessions with the students and teachers and ensuing discussions. It was particularly interesting to see how colleagues at the Council made use of drama sketches in language teaching. (They called themselves by the memorable name of "The Bits and Pieces Theatre Group".) I was also delighted to grab the chance to see something of the city and harbour in crisp winter sunshine. Then before I knew it, it was time to catch the 7.15 a.m. flight to Athens where I was told that one of the Council staff would meet me and accompany me to Ioannina.

At Athens Airport I spotted Paul holding up a card with my name on it. We had not met before, but I recognised him from the description given by one of his colleagues – about forty, medium build, with shortish, dark hair. As I was to discover when we sat in the airport lounge waiting for the onward flight, he had an eye for detail and a good memory.

"I believe I'm right in saying that for your sessions you only need a blackboard or whiteboard and coloured chalk or markers? You don't need an overhead projector or cassette player?"

"That's right," I confirmed. I had with me the handouts for the three-hour talk and workshop with Ioannina University's service English teachers. I had been told that up to twenty teachers might come.

"Everything will be ready for you when we get there. We'll be early so you'll have plenty of time to sort out your papers and things."

He was the epitome of calmness. I felt I could relax, listen to the itinerary and simply carry out the instructions and requests. He was also a considerate host and pleasant companion, and I was pleased that he was responsible for organising my visit. I was in capable hands.

Although I had never been to Ioannina before, I knew from what I had been told in Salonica that the flight would take just over an hour and that some of the mountain scenery would be spectacular. Ioannina lay in the foothills of the Pindus Mountains north-west of Athens; with luck I should be able to get some good views as the weather was bright.

Our flight was called and we boarded. As we walked down the aisle between the rows of double seats, Paul touched my arm. "These are ours," he said, pointing to two on the right. I offered him the window, preferring the aisle, as it gave me more leg room, but he declined, saying I might be able to see something of the view.

"I'd like to have the aisle seat, if it's all right with you," he added. I didn't argue, but sat down and fastened the seat belt. He did the same. I looked out of the window but there was little to see. From the corner of my eye, I noted that Paul was staring straight ahead and gripping his arm rests.

As the plane started to taxi towards the main runway, I noticed that his lips were moving. When we reached the end of it and the engines revved and the plane started to surge, he seemed to sweat, mutter audibly and grip the arms of the seat so tightly that his knuckles stood out white – and his eyes shut. I thought perhaps he was ill. I touched his arm. He jumped and stared at me.

"Are you OK?" I enquired.

"What?" he responded in a strained voice.

I repeated my question. He did not reply but nodded and took up his former tense posture. As soon as the plane was airborne, he looked at his watch and continued to stare at it for two or three minutes. At last he seemed to relax and looked at me with an attempted smile.

"I used to be a pilot," he said conversationally.

I frowned, incredulous. He saw the look on my face.

"Yes, I used to pilot freight," he added.

I stared at him in surprise.

"The trouble is, I know what can go wrong. You can't trust these pilots. That's why I always make sure I get the outside seat. You know, so that you can get out quickly!"

' Christ!' I thought. With him in that state there was no room for *me* to be nervous.

I then listened to a long and detailed explanation of the kind of things that could go wrong on take-off. It ended with Paul saying: "The first three minutes are crucial. If anything's going to happen, it usually happens then. If there's an emergency landing, it's vital to get out as quickly as possible in case of fire."

All this explained the preoccupation with his watch. I closed my eyes and tried to relax. Needless to say, we landed safely at Ioannina, where a car was waiting to take us to the University. It was clouding over and, as we drove towards town, my thoughts were on the return flight late the next morning... and where I was going to sit.

The following Monday I was to give a three-hour session with fourth-year students at Athens University. I had been asked to talk on listening activities as they related to study skills. I had listed my requirements in advance: just a blackboard and students seated so that pair-work and small-group work were possible. I deliberately avoided the need for a cassette recorder or any other equipment in order to keep it simple in case of things failing to materialise or breaking down.

As I had been told that there would be about a hundred students, I had asked to get there early to check out the room and its seating. I preferred to have a semi-circular arrangement and, if necessary, would move the chairs myself; I also wanted to get the first activity ready on the blackboard. Brian, another Council officer, had phoned the University about us coming early and was told that the building was being decorated and the room allotted to me was no longer available. A member of staff would meet us at the entrance and show us where I could go. With a slight feeling of foreboding, I set out to walk the short distance to the University, carrying my briefcase and a bag of handouts.

We were met at the steps by two lecturers, who looked very apologetic. The women introduced themselves and explained that everyone had thought the decorating would be finished the previous week, but there had been delays; as a result, all lecture rooms were in a state of chaos, either with painting half-finished or stacked with furniture from other rooms. There was not one room available that day and, as it was the only time allocated for my session, no alternative day could be arranged. Looking very disappointed, Brian proposed cancelling the session altogether – what other option was there? The University had known of the date and requirements weeks before but had not contacted him about any changes.

I asked the lecturers, Eleni and Maria, if the students had been informed of a cancellation. No, as it was Monday morning there had been no chance to do so. They would all be gathering in the foyer in about twenty minutes' time. I asked to see the foyer. It was a rectangular area which ran into a long carpeted corridor, about ten feet wide, off which several doors led to offices. At the end was a blank wall with narrower passages going round each side.

After a few seconds, I put an impromptu plan to Eleni and Maria. If they could get hold of a portable blackboard to stand against the blank wall, I was willing to go ahead rather than 'disappoint' the students – that is, if they were prepared to sit cross-legged on the carpet down the centre of the corridor. There were nods and smiles at the idea, and the two of them dashed off to find a blackboard. Eleni came back quickly with two chairs, one for me and one for my materials and handouts; she then rejoined Maria in the hunt. I sorted out my papers, discarding some activities that were no longer possible and reorganising the others.

After a few more minutes, they returned, struggling with a heavy blackboard which had no frame or means of support. If it stood on the floor, it could not be seen beyond the first two or three rows when the students sat down. Nor was I prepared to kneel on the floor every time I needed to write on the board. The solution was suggested by Maria: they should balance the board on the two chairs in order to obtain a better height; I would still have to bend to write on it, but at least it would be easier. We tried this, but the board would not stay upright unless held. Eleni and Maria conferred and came up with a solution: they would stand there throughout my session, one on each side of the board, holding it in place; if they got tired, they would crouch down and still hold it upright. We all laughed at the ignominy of the situation, but I gave them heartfelt thanks for saving the session and promised not to use the board excessively; their students, I added, would doubtless enjoy the sight of their lecturers doing some manual work.

When Brian saw that we were ready, he wished us well and said that he would return for lunch but now had to be back in the office.

The students were let in and shown where to sit. The arrangements explained to them by Eleni and Maria caused chaos and laughter. They jostled for position on the carpet, sitting five or six abreast, sometimes more, joking and pushing each other. I asked them to leave a gangway clear down one side so that I could walk down and give handouts and check on group activities.

They enjoyed the novelty of the situation and entered into the spirit of the activities, volunteering and calling out answers and suggestions. Eleni and Maria did stalwart service as blackboard supports. The only untoward incident in an otherwise lively morning was an attempted use of the corridor by staff whose rooms led off it. General amusement greeted the astonished looks on their faces as they manoeuvred through the seated throng, and I had to pause in mid-activity.

There were at least a hundred students that morning – in sharp contrast with the session in Ioannina, when only three teachers had been able to attend. To me it reinforced the conviction always to be flexible and ready for unforeseen circumstances. 'Be prepared' had been my motto for years.

15: As Others See Us: A Postscript

When I look back on the visits I made abroad, I am grateful for such unforgettable experiences. In Finland and Nepal, where I worked longest, I made good friends and still keep in touch. In some of the countries, nothing seems to change over the years – for example, Sierra Leone with its uprisings, resulting in turmoil and hardship. Teaching overseas has given me a greater understanding of different cultures and educational systems. As a result I have become more aware of students' difficulties and needs when they come to study in Britain. There are also rewards in seeing progress and development because of one's efforts. In the Indian sub-continent context, it is flattering to be considered a 'guru'.

An aspect that still interests me is the association between people, places and events within their historical context. An example concerns John Dover Wilson, the literary scholar who became well-known for editing books on Shakespeare in the first half of the 20th century. I recently discovered that in 1906, at the age of twenty-four, he had worked in the University of Helsinki as 'Lektor' for three years, the first Englishman to be appointed to teach English. He also gave private lessons, his most famous student being an officer in the Finnish army –

Mannerheim, who became Marshal of Finland in 1942. While in Finland, Dover Wilson was also Special Correspondent for the *Manchester Guardian* and wrote several anonymous articles about the activities of the Russian Social Revolutionary Party.

As a contrast to my experiences abroad, I thought it would be interesting to see the other side of the coin, so to speak – what impressions, for instance, international students had when they visited Britain. Soon after they arrived to study at Manchester University in October '91, I asked 100 students to write down their first impressions. They were mostly postgraduates with ages ranging from 19 to 55; there were almost equal numbers of men and women. Altogether, 41 countries were represented, but most of the students were from Europe and Asia, with a small number from Africa, Latin America and the Middle East.

The vast majority commented on the city – its architecture and old buildings, large size, busy streets, traffic jams and driving on the left. Also, "so many people live in houses... most built with bricks and the colour red. I wonder what makes people like red... the impression is one is always walking in a village or suburb." The "lovely parks, gardens, trees, flowers and green grass" attracted a number of positive remarks. Understandably, being in the northwest, the "cold, wet, windy, grey, changeable" weather provoked comment. "I'm getting used to carrying all the time an umbrella, to open it for five minutes, to close it again... it is boring." A number of students were surprised at the amount of litter and rubbish in streets. There is "a lot of bright dirt – it's very bright in comparison with dirt in my native town."

Generally, local people were found to be "kind, helpful, polite, friendly, patient and nice", but some found them to be "too busy, rushing around, and reserved". Naturally, there were difficulties with understanding people who "spoke quickly" and in getting used to local accents. One student reflected that "the most strange thing for me even now is that all people speak English. I often realise with great surprise that unconsciously I am always waiting when they will change this strange language and return to the natural one (I mean Russian)."

Anecdotes can add meat to the bare bones of statistical surveys and help to highlight cultural differences and misunderstandings. One

Asian student who had never been outside his country before explained in a puzzled way how he had seen people put a card into a hole in a wall and get money out of it. How could he get one of these cards? Another student told me that she had seen traffic stop at a pedestrian crossing near the University when people pushed a button on the traffic lights. She had never seen such a thing before and stood there for half an hour continually pressing the button and watching the traffic stop. She said it gave her a feeling, previously unknown, of power and control. I wonder what feelings the drivers had!

At the end of one class, a male and female came and asked me about cups and cup sizes. In return, I asked if they were referring to tea cups, coffee cups or was it to do with cookery, comparing a cup of something with a spoonful? The woman looked at me uncomprehendingly; she then asked "how big is cup size A and B and C?" It then dawned on me what she was talking about. "Do you know the word 'brassière' or 'bra'?" "Yes," she replied. So I recommended her to go to a women's underwear shop and ask them to measure her. I was not completely sure that she understood me when she ended by asking "Don't men have cup sizes?" As most teachers will confirm, there is a lot of unintentional humour in ELT which can add to the enjoyment of the work.

Bob Jordan